T0129670

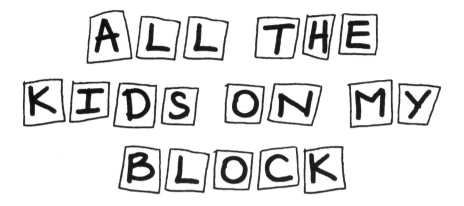

ALL THE KIDS ON MY BLOCK

2nd Edition

David Hoye

WESTBOW
PRESS®
A DIVISION OF THOMAS NELSON
& ZONDERVAN

WestBow Press books may be ordered through booksellers or by contacting:

WestBow Press
A Division of Thomas Nelson & Zondervan
1663 Liberty Drive
Bloomington, IN 47403
www.westbowpress.com
844-714-3454

ISBN: 978-1-6642-9354-0 (sc)
ISBN: 978-1-6642-9355-7 (hc)
ISBN: 978-1-6642-9353-3 (e)

Library of Congress Control Number: 2023903531

Print information available on the last page.

WestBow Press rev. date: 4/10/2023

To my wife, Cheri, and my daughters, Stephanie and Michelle, who always showed patience, love, and understanding while I spent many hours with the children this book is about. I'd also like to thank Theresa Golden, who introduced me to school social work and showed me the sensitivity and caring necessary to connect with kids in school. And special thanks to Marty Wallace, whose skill in play therapy introduced me to a new dimension of working with kids. I'd also like to thank all the talented and caring people with whom I have worked with at Lutheran Social Services and Area Education Agencies 3, 4, and 8. Finally, I give my deepest gratitude and love to all the kids who have inspired this book.

Contents

Introduction

In a time when many new methods of therapy were surfacing, there were times I thought of writing a book about my therapy techniques. The problem was trying to define anything different in my work would be very difficult. It was rather strange, as I knew the work I did with children had some very unique characteristics and, certainly, had been successful throughout the years, but it was hard to define a step-by-step methodology to my therapy. Finally, I came to the realization that it was not what I do with children that was unique and different, but rather, it was the kids I worked with who were all different from one another. Every child I have had the privilege to have a relationship with has their special and unique characteristics that have become my guide in working with them. With this realization, I also discovered that any book I would write would need to be about these kids and how they have directed me, taught me, and molded me into the child-centered person I have become. As difficult as it was to try to outline a book that would describe my therapy techniques, it was just plain simple to outline a book that described the many things "my kids" have taught me throughout the years.

I have had the privilege to work with children from preschool to college age, from bright, talented, and gifted students to those with moderate mental disabilities. I have worked with students with autism, Asperger's syndrome, and Tourette's syndrome. I have worked with kids with visual impairments and those with hearing impairments; others with attention deficit disorder, and those with Down's syndrome. I have had the opportunity to work with those kids who had learning disabilities and those kids with severe developmental delays as well as kids who have been abused, physically and sexually.

I have worked with kids from alcoholic families and with kids who themselves were chemically dependent. I'm sure I have worked with many other disorders or syndromes that affect children. One thing each of my kids had in common was their ability to touch my heart and to have an impact on who I am as a person.

Each in their way has left their indelible mark on Dave Hoye, the school social worker, the therapist, the Christian, and the human being. For this reason, I have chosen some of these special moments and the many lessons these kids have taught me and the philosophy of life I've learned from *All the Kids on My Block*.

School Social Work
as a Profession

School social work is a specialized division of the master in social work program. To be a school social worker, you must have a master's degree in social work from an accredited university. Special course work in working in the schools is part of the curriculum, and a practicum within a school setting is recommended. The school social work specialist certification is available after a certain number of hours as a school social worker within a school setting. This is also highly recommended, as it lends credibility to your practice. I also became a member of the Academy of Certified Social Workers as well as a licensed individual social worker within my state, which allowed me to supervise other social workers and to maintain a private practice if I chose to do so.

I first heard about school social work when I was the area director of Lutheran Social Services in Spencer, Iowa. I was told it was an entry-level position and, in our area, was part of our area education associations. I was led to believe it was predominately an advisory position for the local schools. Later, when I hired a part-time therapist for my agency, the person was currently a school social worker for Area Education Agency 4 out of Sioux Center, Iowa. Bill gave me an entirely different perspective of the duties of a school social worker. Rather than being an entry-level position, it was a job that required a great deal of skills and dealt with pre-K through the twelfth grade. A school social worker required knowledge of all age groups and the ability to work with a multitude of different disabilities. The position also required the ability to work with teachers, administrators, and parents as well as be a liaison within the various communities.

Several years later, I had the opportunity to learn for myself, as I accepted the position of school social worker for Lakeland Area Education Agency out of their Spencer office. It didn't take me long to realize I would need all the tools in my toolbox to be effective in my new job. My position was typical within the agency, with four school districts encompassing thirteen buildings. At the time most of the schools had high school counselors but no elementary counselors. The AEA social worker often was expected to maintain counseling relationships with the regular education population as well as the special education students. This often included classroom time together with the regular teacher helping students learn social skills and communication skills.

I quickly found out being a school social worker was not a nine-to-five job. It often included early morning team meetings, starting at 7:30 a.m., and afternoon staffings and IEP meetings, which easily could last until 6:00 p.m. The school social worker was part of building teams that included a school psychologist, a special education consultant, a speech and language pathologist, and at times hearing specialists, occupational therapists, and a physical therapist. The teams also included the building principal and guidance counselor as well as the special education teachers. Each team was an integral part of dealing with student problems in each building. I found out early on it took wearing several different caps to be effective in my job.

The districts being served could be as close as in the town where the office was or up to forty-five miles from your office. Driving also became a normal part of the job as well as finding a way to serve thirteen buildings effectively in a five-day week. If it seemed complicated, it certainly was.

Interestingly, AEA employees did not work directly for any of their individual schools but rather for the educational agency. This gave them the flexibility and latitude to act as advocates for their students and families and at times be in opposition to the administration or teachers in the schools they worked at. Mediation and negotiation skills were important to work within the parameters of your districts and still act as advocates for your students and parents. Most administrators acknowledged the AEA teams needed independence from the districts to be effective in their jobs.

The school social worker was always a member of the district crisis teams and needed to be available in the possibility of any number of explosive situations that could affect the district at any time during the day. These teams usually met weekly or as needed to help be prepared when emergencies would happen. Because of this, it took the understanding from all the schools that at times the school social worker could be called away from assigned times in each of the buildings. It was very important to have a good relationship with all school secretaries so they would understand the need for flexibility in the schedules and run interference for you when the schedules were suddenly changed. Many times school secretaries helped ensure my relationships within the buildings by helping the staff understand the nature of emergencies within my schools.

The school social worker is also often involved in community activities and committees having to do with social work. I was involved in the Committee for the Prevention of Child Abuse in one community and was also involved in several county protection teams that dealt with child abuse in their individual counties. I also gave many presentations on attention deficit disorder, suicide prevention, and social work in rural settings as well as presentations on grief and loss.

I also did support groups for parents of children with attention deficit disorder as well as for parents of children with autism and parents of kids identified as explosive children. I did a five-week training class for teachers learning to deal with the explosive child. This course followed the guidelines set by Ross Green, the author of *The Explosive Child*.

The school social work position can be done with as little or as much actual contact with children and families as wanted by the individual. School social workers who want to be primarily consultants with the schools can be limited in their contact with children and families. They often go only to IEP meetings or other school staffings. School social workers who choose to have contact with families, kids, teachers, and administrators will often see kids in individual or group settings and will have contact with families in their homes as well as at the school. Acting as an intermediary between the school and family is much easier if you have a relationship not only with the child but also with their family. It is also important to know your teachers and administrators well and to gain their trust, as you are working with the kids in their care. It certainly is more difficult to be active with kids and families, but it lends more credibility when negotiating between the schools and families to be seen as an advocate for the families as well as a supporter for the teachers and school. The school social worker who acts primarily as a consultant is easily perceived as only caring about the interests of the school. Both paths of school social work and any combination of the two can be effective in a school setting. The hands-on approach seems to have more benefits yet at the same time has more risks. Being involved with kids and their families as well as establishing trusting relationships with teachers and administrators can take a lot of relationship-building as well as mediating between the two groups so they all have a trusting relationship with you.

School social workers have a different role than school counselors but work very closely with them. They are there for consultation and collaboration. At times counselors and social workers facilitate groups together and will do home visits together with families of kids with whom they are both involved.

School social workers have special education students as their primary population but will also work with at-risk students and those who have behavior problems but are not in special education. Because school social workers have several schools, they depend on the building counselor for updates and current information about families. Their coordination with staff and at-risk personnel keeps all staff working together in the same direction with the families they serve. The school social worker is also an important member of the building team with other representatives, such as speech clinicians, consultants, and school psychologists, who weekly collaborate on the needs and strategies for working with the special education population.

You can see those people who considered school social work as an entry-level position for MSW graduates had no real understanding of either the function or complexity of the job. To be an effective school social worker, it is necessary to have a wide variety of experience with children of all age levels. It also is mandatory to have an understanding of the different learning disabilities as well as learning styles. A school social worker also needs to be able to and willing to work with multiple levels of developmental disabilities and delays that need a special knowledge as well as a great deal of compassion and patience. It can be an overwhelming profession unless the person is fully developed in their skills of working with all children as well as parents and administrators. On the other hand, I cannot think of a profession more rewarding if done effectively.

School social workers can also be hired by individual school districts to work either throughout the entire district or only in an individual building or grade level. The dynamics change dramatically when the district determines the priorities for the work to be done by the school social worker. If the social worker is working for the entire district, then he/she will be supervised by the building principal at each level, and the duties will be determined by the needs of each individual building or grade level. The social worker is still likely to be building teams, but the teams could vary from building to building and be very different from the roles of AEA teams in the social worker's various buildings. For example, in a high school, the team could consist of the building principal, the guidance counselor, and any at-risk director. At times workers from other disciplines would not necessarily be on the team with the social worker. Other differences include the lack of independence when working for only one district or building. The school social worker would have a lot less ability to determine the needs of his/her building and to decide the best areas for him/her to work to be successful with the students in that building. If the school social worker is in several buildings, there will be times when there will be competition for his/her time and services by the principals of each individual building. Some advantages would be the limited amount of travel involved and less people to be accountable to. Each principal could determine the amount of independence allowed in their building, depending on their confidence in your ability to determine what services would be most beneficial to their students.

Difference of opinions with supervisors could be much more difficult to resolve, as those supervisors determine much of what is considered appropriate and OK for you to disagree with. Advocating for parents or students can become much more difficult if the building principal takes the side of teachers or administration rather than that of the students or parents, and the school social worker is expected to agree with their supervisors. A great deal of difficulty could occur if the social worker continued their disagreement with others that the administration agreed with. It would take superb negotiating and mediating skills to be able to advocate for students and parents under those circumstances.

In all the different scenarios for the school social worker, special education is a priority and much of their time is spent with the students with special needs and their families. Whether the social worker is working for an area education agency, another cooperative agency, individual schools, or as a private contractor, their funding usually comes from special education dollars. The value of a good school social worker comes from their ability to navigate through difficult circumstances and still be effective in serving their schools and the kids and their families.

The profession of school social work gives many opportunities to make a difference in the lives of students and their families as well as being able to positively affect the culture of the schools in which they work. It takes a skilled clinician to be able to work with a wide age range of students and with multiple special needs of those students. Having the ability to connect with students and their families as well as teachers and administrators within the school districts is a necessary tool each school social worker needs to have to be effective. Schools that have learned the value of school social work have opened the doors to many positive accomplishments within their districts. Compassion, care, and sensitivity to needs are only part of what a social worker brings to their schools.

They also bring the ability to help all sides be able to see things from the other person's perspective and to consider making changes in how they deal with situations. From hostility and doubt, the school social worker can help establish understanding and trust. That goes a long way in solving difficulties within the school setting. This is just a snapshot of what a school social worker does and the needed assistance they can bring to their schools.

Chapter One
Study and Discussion Guide

1. Name the educational requirements to become a school social worker.
2. In what ways is it beneficial for a school district to have a school social worker as part of their educational team?
3. Why is special education the primary focus for school social workers?
4. Discuss the relationship between school social workers and the district guidance counselors.
5. How are school social workers helpful to families and students in their relationships with administrators and teachers?

What All Kids
Need from Us

A major part of this book revolves around the kids I have worked with during my days as a school social worker and with those kids whom I had in therapy. This chapter is about all the kids in each of our lives we have had the privilege to work with and the knowledge of what all kids need in their lives to become successful and fulfilled adults who make their positive mark in our society. I will divide this chapter into categories. These are areas we, adults, need to provide for our kids.

A Sense of Belonging

All of us have a need for a sense of belonging to know we are all right and OK in the world we work, play, and live. Without feeling that we belong, there would be a sense of emptiness and of being alone. Just knowing we belong to our family, our social group, our sports teams, our coworkers, or our church groups can give us what we need to know about ourselves and our self-esteem. As parents, we need to show our children, our spouses, and our friends that our family is important to us, and we need to make the effort to spend time and emotional involvement with each member so each of us has that connectedness with one another and can know that feeling of support that comes with it.

As teachers and educators, we need to know the kids in our class and to recognize those who seem to fit in the larger classroom group and those who seem distant and apart from the group. It is even more important to know our kids well enough to see how they connect with one another outside the structure of the classroom.

Those of us who work in the schools know if kids don't get that sense of belonging at home, then each of us needs to make efforts to help them find some sense of belonging at school. Whether it is sports, clubs, or outside activities, kids need to have that sense of belonging somewhere. Unfortunately, those kids who cannot connect either at home or at school are at risk for joining gangs or being drawn into cults. They can become loners who drop out of school and sometimes drop out of life. If there was ever an opportunity to help kids, it's there for us to find a way that each child can find their strengths. Then we can help them find a place where they can fit. Sometimes the only connection they have can be our relationship with them. Without some connectedness, those kids can be lost.

Consistency

All our kids would benefit from consistency in all areas of their lives. As a matter of fact, all adults would benefit as well. Unfortunately, that's probably not going to happen in all facets of our lives. As adults in the lives of children, we can make a difference by providing the same atmosphere and the same level of treatment and the same manner of discipline to all the kids we work with daily. This isn't saying we can't have a bad day, but then we can just tell our kids we're having a bad day and it isn't their fault. What kids need to know is we will treat them all with respect and dignity every day and in all that we do together. This is true at home, in school, in sports, in clubs, and in any other activity. Kids have the right to know they can depend on us to treat them fairly and decently in all they do. They should not be humiliated, put down, made fun of, or be the butt end of anyone's jokes. They should not be singled out nor disciplined in front of the whole group. If these things alone could be changed, the self- esteem of all our kids would certainly be improved a great deal.

At home, parents need to be together and consistent in their parenting style. Over the years I'm sure I have taught at least a dozen parenting programs, and I am aware of many others. All have their positive aspects, and parents just need to find one that works for them. The key to any effective parenting program is that the parents use it together. If the parents agree on a program, then it is much easier to get the kids to buy into it. Unless it is done with consistency, it just will not be effective. We go back to that word, *consistency*, again. Our kids will always respond to consistency in whatever we are working with them on.

In sports or other organization, where more than one coach or leader work with the kids, the coaches and leaders of the group need to let the kids know their leadership styles. Kids need to know, although they may lead in somewhat different styles, the consistency and goals for the kids remain the same. If the leaders treat any of the kids differently than others, it will destroy the trust they have with their team or group.

Responsibility

Kids don't become responsible on their own, and a work ethic doesn't appear without help from the adults in their lives. At home, teaching responsibility can begin at a young age. Kids can be introduced to age-appropriate chores or household duties by their parents by teaching and modeling the chores the kids will be expected to accomplish. Each family can decide on the level of chores for their different aged children and can decide whether their kids will receive allowances or be doing the chore just as part of the family. How the chores are assigned and whether to use chore charts or lists to help the kids accomplish what is expected of them is up to each family.

Parents need to be very cautious in assigning tasks and need to give positive reinforcement and praise when they have done their assigned work. Parents cannot be critical in teaching or reteaching a skill. They need patience and the ability to assure their kids that their effort is appreciated. If parents are overly critical or verbally insulting to the kids, not only will they refuse or avoid chores, but they will also run from all other responsibility at home, at school, at work, or in sports. When kids learn responsibility from their parents at home, it often will carry over into their school and even into their sports and work experiences. For those kids who have not learned responsibility at home, it makes it very difficult to take responsibility for expectations in other aspects of their lives. These are the kids who need the other adults in their lives to step up to the plate and to help them learn responsibility by mentoring and teaching them in school, at work, or in sports. Many times bosses at work and coaches in their sports have little patience with those kids who are not responsible to their peers or their coworkers or their teammates. Much of the burden for teaching the child responsibility rests with classroom teachers, peer mentors, or other special people in the school, such as custodians, bus drivers, cooks, secretaries, or any adult who is able and willing to take the time to make a difference with our kids. All kids want to be successful and to be able to compete with their peers academically and in extracurricular activities. The best way to help these kids accept responsibility is to show them you care enough to help make a difference for them.

It's not that kids want to be irresponsible or like being put down, but rather, it is because they haven't learned how to be responsible. It's interesting how quickly a child can learn when they know someone cares enough to help and teach them. When a child wants to please an adult who cares, they are willing to and can do what the special adults want them to do. Then, and only then, can they generalize what they have learned, taking it into the classroom and onto the playing field. Responsibility does not come to kids through osmosis nor by a magic wand. It only comes when someone is willing to teach them.

Self-Confidence

All adults need to be part of confidence-building with their children and can make a difference in their world by giving them an opportunity to be successful in life. Kids need to be nurtured and praised as a way of letting them know when they are successful. Confidence does not come without trial and error, and making mistakes can help them attain a sense of accomplishment by knowing how to correct their mistake and become better at what they are doing. Adults may be the catalyst to help a child become confident, but somewhere in the transition process, the kids need to feel it on their own and be able to build on it through their successes.

I think it is important that kids are given opportunities in areas of their strength early on in their development. This can be true, be it in sports, science, woodworking, hunting, or any other activity the child enjoys and can become successful in.

Self-confidence does not mean an obsession with certain activities but rather can lead to success in different areas that build from the confidence of their first area of success. A confident soccer player may become a successful placekicker on a football team. A quarterback in football often becomes the point guard in basketball and the pitcher on their baseball team. A setter in volleyball can also excel in basketball and in softball. Yes, they need to be excellent athletes, but success in the one area can give them the confidence to gain that success in another area. A kid who has success on a Lego robotic team can carry that scientific confidence into high school science club, which can eventually lead to a career choice he may not otherwise have chosen.

There is a big difference between being confident and becoming cocky or self-centered. Adults in kids' lives can teach them the difference. Ability is of no use if fair play and sportsmanship are not part of their beliefs. Losing and making mistakes take a confident kid to handle it well and to learn from it. I had the opportunity to coach little league baseball and softball for about twelve years and was able to see how parents and coaches could make a difference with kids and help them learn the game.

To work with the younger kids can be very rewarding, as they learn step by step how to play the game and begin to gain confidence. I also was a high school softball coach for sixteen years and was able to see the girls at a more advanced level than the younger kids. I think parents and coaches can play an even more important role in the lives of their athletes through learning not just winning or losing but also the life skills it takes to be successful in any area. It was very heartwarming to see a young lady with average skills become a better player through hard work and dedication.

It was also very heartwarming to coach the excellent athlete and to watch them learn the life value that the team came first above any individual awards. A combination of humility, excellence on the field, and having fun are attributes they can build on for the rest of their lives. Unfortunately, in the coaching profession, you see those coaches who criticize and belittle and treat the players horribly, all in the name of winning. It's hard to watch any child be torn down by an adult and watch their self-confidence wither away.

Whether with our young children or our high school athletes or those who excel in speech or drama or debate, how they are taught and treated by the adults in their lives can make the difference between self-confident adults and those with negative feelings about themselves or their abilities. For our children, we as adults have an obligation to build and nurture their confidence in whatever area they choose to participate in.

When we all nurture our kids and guide them in their development, we will be amazed at the wonderful gifts they give to us with their love, their humor, and their unique qualities. In the latter part of my career in the schools, I had the opportunity to help develop a program called "Positive Behavior Supports." It is a program where every component of a school and community must work together to nurture and change the climate of the school. One small aspect of it is called catching kids doing things right. The statistics show, for every single negative, a child needs four positives to gain in self-worth and confidence. All those little things we may pass over or say, "Why should I praise a student for doing what is expected of him?" The answer is we all respond to receiving positives from others. It's a program that will benefit any organization that puts it into place. In the chapters to come, I will share some poignant stories about the wonderful transition of kids from being lost and forgotten to being more of a success in life.

Chapter Two
Study and Discussion Guide

1. Name the basic needs all kids must meet to be successful.
2. If those needs are not met, describe some of the potential negative results.
3. Success in one often leads to the same in another area. Describe why this may happen.
4. What is the importance of a positive adult relationship in a child's life?
5. Negative attitudes can have a lasting impact on how a child feels about himself. Tell some of the ways this can happen.

THREE

Wisdom: The Philosophy of Kids

Never have I found greater wisdom than in the mind of a child. Kids have a tremendous knack of interpreting their world in a way that makes sense to them and helps them cope with its obstacles in very different and creative ways. What seems to take forever for adults to struggle with, the philosophy of kids swiftly and easily directs them in their answers. I think we, adults, spend so much time complicating and dissecting our philosophy of life that it is barely recognizable when the time for action has come. Kids, on the other hand, simplify their solutions to problems by having a simple, clear-cut, common-sense philosophy in dealing with life. Some of the wisdom of kids come out of necessity. They have learned to adapt to their surroundings and to cope with their daily problems. Kids who deal with abuse daily learn to avoid or appease their abuser. Kids who deal with parent's anger learn to be peacemakers. Kids with absent parents learn to be substitute parents for their younger siblings.

Unfortunately, kids' philosophy is not always healthy for them, but it always is practical in dealing with their difficulties. Overall, the simple philosophy of life our kids develop can teach us a great deal about coping skills and about problem-solving. It can also help us understand why kids react the way they do to parents, teachers, and even their peers.

Kids view their lives through the eyes of others. If parents treat their children as if they were incapable, the kids will develop a philosophy that will live down to those negative expectations. If a child cannot please their parents, they will sometimes set themselves up for not pleasing other adults in their lives so they maintain the image they have been given. Although this seems like negative coping, kids who develop this philosophy do so out of self-protection and preservation. If they please their teachers, it will only make their parents angry for proving them wrong, so it's easier to go with the flow. Although a negative philosophy such as this can lead to destructive outcomes, the kids will use it because it works for the moment.

Another example of kids' philosophy deals with lying. Ask any kid why they lie, and they will tell you "to avoid the consequences." Even though they know the consequences will eventually come, lying delays it from happening. Lying is not a moral issue with kids; it's a practical one. If I tell the truth, I'm immediately in trouble. If I lie, I don't get into trouble now, and maybe I will get away with it. Avoidance of negative consequences is something we all attempt to do. Adults, however, use complicated ways of diluting or exaggerating the truth so the deception will not be considered a lie. They still are able avoid the dreaded consequences. Kids are simply more honest in their deception and don't make any complicated excuses for their lies. They just lie to delay consequences. At times, in school and at home, adults spend a great deal of time worrying about their children who have lied. Rather than deal with the act as the child sees it, we complicate it with moral issues and concerns over the child's lack of conscience or guilt over their lying. When the child's lying becomes the focus, we have reinforced the child's reason for lying in the first place—delaying the consequence. When we realize that simple honest philosophy of lying, it's no longer a big deal, and we can deal out the consequences and reinforce that lying doesn't have enough benefit to outweigh the consequences, and then it is no longer an issue.

Another example of kids' philosophy is their attitude toward their friends. Kids develop a philosophy of trust for their friends that circumvents any difficulties they have with one another. Parents are often confused by their child's anger at a friend one day and their close friendship the next day. Kids' philosophy says friends can get mad at one another, but that doesn't mean they're not still friends. This philosophy is found much more with boys than with girls. Girls have a little more difficulty with their loyalty of friendship. Boys expect to get mad at one another and to fight and squabble, but that's just part of being boys. They can't understand why people would doubt their friendship or be surprised they were still together after seeing them get mad at one another. I remember, growing up, the battles and bickering I did with my buddies. Yet that was all forgotten the next day. We never doubted our friendship. As kids get older, this philosophy changes somewhat, but boys always seem to handle their differences and little battles without it hurting their friendship. This simple philosophy of "just because we're friends doesn't mean we get along all the time" is very dominant with boys in the elementary school. It is also the basis for a healthy way of dealing with relationships and not expecting people to be perfect or always trying to please.

Kids often don't want to continue in many activities because of the following philosophy. Kids say, "If it doesn't work the first time, why keep trying, because it won't get better." Whether it is piano lessons, cleaning their rooms, doing time tests in school, playing sports, or doing dishes, if it isn't worth doing today, it sure won't be worth doing tomorrow. Rather than being a defeatist attitude, this philosophy is very practical and simplistic. Why waste our time and effort on something that probably won't work. So if we wonder why we get resistance to our thinking of "once you start something, you need to finish it," that's why. There are times it may be worth the ensuing struggle to battle this philosophy, but often it will be a waste energy and be very frustrating. It is important to ensure early success for our kids when they encounter something new. If kids experience early success, then their need for the "why-waste-my-time philosophy" is no longer there.

The following examples typify kids' philosophies and the wisdom behind them. In no way does this exhaust all their methods of dealing with life. I have compiled what I call the ABCs of kids' philosophy.

A is for Attitude—Kids' philosophy says attitude is what parents and teachers say kids have. Kids don't consider attitude as something they claim or possess. It also isn't something they consider with their peers. Attitude is an adult thing to be lightly regarded and not to be taken seriously.

A is also for Age—Kids' philosophy is no age is a good age. There is always someone older who gets more privileges and someone younger who gets more attention. Whatever the age, you're always too young or too old, and you either did it last year or you have to wait 'til next year. Some significant exceptions are age sixteen, when you can get a driver's license; age eighteen, when you are considered an adult; and age twenty-one, when you become legal.

B is for Bad—Kids say bad is anything isn't good. If good is receiving As and Bs, then bad must be Cs or lower in school. If good is paying attention in school, then bad is being distracted, not paying attention, or creating disruption. If being good is always doing chores, cleaning your room, or being on time, then bad must be not doing chores, leaving a messy room, and always being late. Are we seeing a pattern here? Kids' philosophy sees only black or white, right or wrong, and nothing in between. In other words, if you aren't considered good, then you must be bad.

C is for Clown—Kids' philosophy says being a clown always gets you attention. Often it makes you the center of attraction. Being a clown allows you to get a lot of laughs and distracts from all the negative feelings you might be having. If you're not doing well in school, you might as well have fun, and being a clown is an excellent way to have fun. A clown always seems to be liked and is surrounded by friends. Unfortunately, the attention eventually becomes negative and doesn't help how you are doing in school. But your friends don't care because as much as they laugh, you're the one who gets in trouble.

C is also for Caring—Kids have a tremendous gift of caring for those who need caring in the worst way, whether it is bringing home a stray cat or dog or going to a nursing home to cheer up the residents by reading to them. Under their cover of never being sensitive to anyone except themselves is this wonderful large heart that cares for others.

D is for Disadvantaged—Kids' philosophy says if you "ain't smart," then you must be disadvantaged when compared to other kids. Unfortunately, being disadvantaged means they are different from other kids. Being disadvantaged encompasses not doing well in school, not getting work done, not being prompt, or losing your materials or your way. When kids are disadvantaged, they feel different from other kids. Usually, that is OK. If they don't want to feel less competent than other kids, then they will get into trouble and deal with those consequences.

E is for Effort—Kids' philosophy says effort is only what you need to get you where you want to go. Kids will differ in their output of energy and effort in relationship to the significance and importance to them of their goals. Kids' view of effort should not be mistaken for expectations of effort from parents, teachers, coaches, or even friends. Although some kids are pleasers and will try put in the effort expected of them from others, most will set their standards or effort to fit their needs.

F is for Friendship—Kids' philosophy says friendship is the most important thing in their lives. Only their family or their faith may rival friendship. Friendship encompasses three categories: best friends, good friends, and sometimes friends. Kids can always tell you who fits into each category. Sometimes "wanna be friends" is another category for kids who want to be your friends or kids you want to be friends with.

F is also for Future—Kids' philosophy says the future can be the rest of our lives or the next five minutes, depending on their needs at the moment. Kids have the amazing capacity to use their entire energy supply on the next five minutes as if their lives depended on it. Equally amazing is they can dream and plan and scheme for what the entire rest of their lives will be. They can use the world of fantasy and of dreams and hope as they look boldly into their future. They also can have extreme funnel vision and deal only with the now. The future, for kids, allows them to be just kids and to think of the happily-ever-after and the positive outcomes for their dreams.

G is for Good—Kids' philosophy says good is simply the opposite of bad. Good is doing all those things you're supposed to do and pleasing all the people you are supposed to please. Good is smart, it is right, it is on time, it is always happy, it is always pleasant, and it is always polite. Good is a lot harder than bad!

H is for Hero—Kids' philosophy says a hero is someone you imitate and be like. Although most kids will have heroes like sport stars or musical stars, the real heroes for kids are their parents, their siblings, or other relatives. On occasion, it will be an older student in their school or a teacher or a coach. Kids pick their mystical hero at times to impress other kids, while their real hero, they keep to themselves. Look at interviews of seniors in high school and see their answers when asked who has been most influential in their lives. It most always is one of their parents. It is necessary for us as parents to know this when we look at ourselves as role models and set standards for our kids. Do they follow what we do or what we say?

I is for Image—Kids' philosophy says image is everything and image is nothing. It also can change from one moment to the next. As important as peer pressure and belonging to the group is for kids, their image is one of the few things they have control over. It is something they can choose, so it is a form of independence. No, parents, it is not just a means of rebelling. The image kids want to project can change according to each individual and to every situation. I have been amazed at kids with long hair who suddenly cut it short, not because everyone's on their case, but for some other reason only they know.

J is for Joke—Kids' philosophy says joke is anything they think is funny, not to be confused with really being funny. Telling jokes is a learning experience for kids as they discover their sense of humor. Kids will often laugh when they don't understand just because others are laughing. Kids also have difficulty with appropriateness of jokes and whom share them with. Again, this is a trial-and-error experience for them and should be redirected rather than be discouraged.

J is also for Journey - Journey for a kid can be their next day in school, or a trip across the country, or a fantasy in their minds. The journey of life would be looked at one day at a time, and their expectations or fantasies may or may not come true.

K is for Kids—Kids' philosophy says a kid is anyone younger than they are. They say kids can be OK, but they also can be "pesty" or "a pain." It's all right to have little kids look up to you and "hang around." They are not to be confused with friends. It's almost never OK to call a kid a "kid." That makes them feel looked down upon. The most likely time a kid will accept that name is when his parents are expecting something from him. Then you may hear, "What do you expect? I'm only a kid."

L is for Learning—Kids' philosophy is learning is anything teachers think you should know and parents want you to know, not to be confused with something that may have value or interest to you. When learning is something that has interests for them and helps them know more about something they like, then it can be all right.

M is for Money—Kids' philosophy says money is only important when you need it to buy what you want, and you can't con your folks out of it.

Money becomes much more important for a teenager when dates and cars enter the picture. Money and earning money, however, often have different levels of importance, and the more money a teenager has, the more likely they are to realize what they really need.

N is for Nicknames—Kids' philosophy says nicknames can be all right, depending on who knows them and who is calling you by that name. There are good nicknames and bad nicknames and nicknames that are OK for some people to call you but not for others. Some nicknames that sound offensive are really endearing for them. Others that sound quite harmless can start a fight in a minute. It is not confusing to the kids, but it will frustrate adults trying to figure it out.

O is for Old—Kids' philosophy says old is anyone older than twenty-five. Over thirty now qualifies as ancient. Fifty and over is considered prehistoric. Old is also any food over a day old, any clothes have been worn and not liked, and any music isn't current, except for remakes they don't know are remakes. Exceptions to old are favorite clothes, particularly jeans; cars that belong to them; and certain celebrities over the age of twenty-five who do not act over the age of twenty-five. Sound confusing?

P is for Party—Kids say parties are any gathering of friends, anytime, anywhere. Parents need to realize party often means alcoholic beverages or drugs but does not have to be. Many of our nondrinking kids still use the term *party*, and our younger kids have picked up the term *party* from birthday parties, etc.

Q is for Quiet—Kids' philosophy says if it's quiet, then it must be boring. Their interpretation of quiet is completely different from that of their parents and other adults. What we consider blasting out our eardrums is often considered pleasant to kids. When we say keep it down to a mild roar, they consider that too quiet. In a world full of decibels, most kids have not learned to appreciate quiet. However, if there is a time they need to rest or want complete quiet, they are intolerable of the slightest noise by their siblings or parents.

R is for Real—Kids' philosophy says real is anything within the realm of their imaginations, dreams, and plans. Adults confuse kids' realities with purposeful lying or storytelling. A kid's wishes can become his realities. They are not always negative or aberrant-thinking. Their perception of reality often softens the blows of what is real within their lives. It is often the catalyst to achievement in making these wishes or fantasies come true. We, adults, are often too critical of kids' reality, and we need to put it into perspective of their developmental age and their abilities. Kids' realities need these dreams and wishes, and they should not be crushed and demolished by unthinking adults.

S is for Space—Kids' philosophy says space is any amount of distance they need to feel safe or respected. That distance can vary from a few feet to a much larger area. Kids need their individual space, where they live, where they go to school, and where they play. At home, if a child has his room, it needs to be his safe place and not to be unduly violated by siblings, parents, or guests in the house. If rooms are shared, there needs to be those unmarked but well-defined perimeters for each kid in the room. At school, the child's desk and locker need to be their space; teachers and other kids need to respect that space and not violate it. When a kid says, "Get out of my face," you know you're in their space. Teachers who have the best relationships with kids know the secret of not violating their space even when disciplining or correcting. When kids play, they have a definition of space that tells others what's OK and what isn't. We, adults, need to be sensitive to the need for space by our kids, just as we want our space protected and honored.

T is for Trust—Kids' philosophy says trust is the most important element in any relationship, and it does not just happen but must be earned. Young children often trust very quickly and openly. They soon learn trust is often violated or misused by their peers and, unfortunately, even at times by adults. Is it any wonder why stepfamilies have difficulties when the stepparent comes into the family and automatically assumes he will be trusted and given authority with the kids? Unfortunately, kids feel trust has already been violated by the divorce. They are not about to take the risk of trusting again. A whole chapter could be devoted to kids' feelings on trust and mistrust but suffice in saying gaining their trust is important in relating to them. It also explains why kids are so reluctant to "narc or squeal" on their friends, even when they know what their friends are doing is wrong. It takes a very strong relationship with parents and other adults for the child to risk revealing any secrets or pacts they have with their friends, even when they are illegal or life-threatening. On the other hand, I have discovered, from the many kids I have worked with, once trust has been earned, it has created a strong bond in our relationship.

U is for Understanding—Kids' philosophy says understanding is something that takes time and effort on the part of the kids and adults. Being understood is very important for kids. Achieving it, however, can be difficult because kids don't always understand what they desperately want others to. They also have difficulty verbalizing their feelings when they want to be understood. Understanding kids means taking the time to really listen to them and to watch for all their nonverbal ways of telling you how they feel. It also means checking out how they are feeling rather than making assumptions. Kids want to understand as well as to be understood. We need to be patient and explain slowly and clearly how we feel. An understanding between kids and adults can be a wonderful catalyst for a good relationship, and it is worth our time and effort. Remember, for kids, understanding becomes synonymous with caring, so its importance cannot be overstated.

V is for Vacation—Kids' philosophy says vacation is any time or place when they don't have to go to school. Kids don't need a long vacation away from home, going to exotic places, but rather, they need a time to spend with family and friends and doing things that have real meaning to them. It also can be anytime when they can just relax and be free from some responsibilities. Time spent is far more important to kids than where they spend it. For parents, vacations for their kids can be a time to encourage their hobbies and their talent. Little league, sports, 4H, camps, and other organized activities can be good for our kids, but having their parents there to watch and help is what is important to them. As much as kids like to tell the places they have gone to, usually, the importance of these vacations become clear when you listen to the kids talk about who they did things with and the relationship value of the time spent on vacations.

W is for Wish—Kids' philosophy says a wish is the way you would really like things to be. At times their wishes are to have their parents back together after a divorce. Other times it is to have Grandma or Grandpa still be alive. A wish can be as simple as wanting an ice cream cone on a hot summer day or a friend to play with when they are lonely. It also could be as complicated as a detailed plan for their lives or a dramatic change in their world. A wish for a kid is more than a passing daydream yet less than an obsession and somewhere in the middle. It is usually harmless and wishful adventure for them. There are times, however, when it can be a way of avoiding acceptance of the way things really are.

X is for X-tra—Kids' philosophy says X-tra is anything more than what they really want to do. This is not to be confused with what others want them to do. What is normal and acceptable to some kids may be seen as X-tra for others. Sometimes what kids are willing to do may be far more than what others expect from them.

Y is for Yesterday—Kids' philosophy says yesterday always seems different from what it really was. Kids have the remarkable trait of selective memory. They choose often to block out the unpleasant and to embellish the positive things. When kids are asked to remember what they did, they often cannot tell you. However, when kids mention their memories themselves, the details they can recall of the experiences they perceived are amazing.

Z is for Zero—Kids' philosophy says zero is how adults rate on a scale of 1 to 100 when they try to placate or pacify rather than listen. Zero is also for people who think they know what kids need and want without ever asking for their input.

Well, that's the ABCs of kids' philosophy. Although this is certainly only a glimpse at how kids feel and react, it does give us a taste of how kids look differently at life than adults do. There is a lot of wisdom in how they perceive their world and how they learn to cope with those things they cannot change. For kids, it often seems like they have very little control over anything. I have found over the years kids' philosophy is not nearly as different as it first appears. We can certainly see when we look a little deeper into the reasons for it. It's then we can see the wisdom kids show in many of the things they say and do. There certainly is a reason behind their philosophy, and we need to have the wisdom they do in learning what life is all about and what they want from the adults in their lives.

Chapter Three
Study and Discussion Guide

1. Discuss the simplicity of kid's philosophy.
2. What are the three areas of kid's philosophy that are difficult for parents to understand?
3. How can kids' simple philosophy be unhealthy for them?
4. Talk about the author's ABCs of kids' philosophy.
5. Name some of the differences between kids' philosophy and that of their parents or other adults.
6. The ABCs of kids' philosophy is only this author's perception. In what ways do you agree or disagree with his simplified look at how kids look at life.

FOUR

Education: The Many Lessons I Have Learned from Kids

Let me preface this chapter by acknowledging I am not a teacher by trade. I am a counselor, therapist, and social worker. Working in the field of education has been a whole new learning experience for me. I have become intertwined with the education process and have been blessed with time in the classroom as well as with students individually and in groups. I have learned a great deal from classroom teachers, but most of my education has come from the kids. Many of the kids I have worked with have educational, behavioral, or developmental disabilities; yet they have been master teachers to me in areas I never would have dreamed possible. This chapter is designed to explore some of the wonderful experiences in learning I have shared with my students and the context in which they have happened.

A great many of the students I have seen throughout the years have had a series of failures, academically and socially. They generally feel they are incompetent or naughty or bad. They feel they are not successful in much of anything. One of the things I would always try to do when working with students was to find something each one of these kids were good at. I strongly believe every human being has been blessed with many gifts.

However, most of these kids were at a point where they couldn't see their strengths. I would always attempt to find those strengths and to empower them to feel the experience of success. In doing this, I was continually amazed at the terrific talents and abilities these kids have and how willing they are to share them. Once they believed I was sincere in my interest in them, they shared openly.

I have learned a lot about strength, courage, and humility but also about loyalty, resilience, persistence, and humor. In addition, I have read poetry, short stories, cartoons, songs, and journals that revealed talent neither the child nor I knew existed. I have been taught how to milk cows, how to show horses, cows, pigs, and sheep. I have learned how to play cribbage, Yahtzee, bridge, pinochle, chess, and many other games my kids have been willing to teach me. I have learned about welding, fishing, roping, baseball, and soccer as well as many other sports and activities. This was all because I wouldn't believe these kids had no talents or abilities. I also encouraged them to share those abilities with me and to be willing to teach me as well. I will share with you some of the humorous moments as well as some poignant stories of some wonderful kids who have touched my heart with their gifts.

A group I worked with for several years taught me a great deal about honesty, courage, and loyalty. This group also taught me kids need to believe in themselves and one another to survive and thrive in a sometimes dangerous and hostile world. This group was high school students who had been through treatment for drugs and/or alcohol addiction and had returned to their home setting for after-care and rehabilitation. The group was designed to provide support for these students in the school setting. It was to reinforce after-care programs they were involved in (AA, ADTU, counseling). These kids mostly came voluntarily, though at times they were referred by their treatment center, juvenile probation, or the Department of Human Services. Even though these kids have just returned from a positive environment, they were still very fragile and vulnerable in terms of their sobriety. During the years I helped facilitate this group, the recidivism and relapse rate was certainly higher than most dependent adults. The difficulty in handling their addiction was not only in their acceptance of their problems, but also in convincing families, friends, and teachers that they were, indeed, alcoholics and could never drink or use again in their lives without losing what they had gained in treatment. It's tough enough for a sixteen-year-old to accept they can never again consume alcoholic beverages or addictive drugs, but it becomes ten times tougher when the community around them does not treat their addiction seriously. Even adult alcoholics often have trouble understanding that kids could be addicted and, hence, are not always supportive to them.

Given this background, it took tremendous courage for these kids to face their peers and classmates and to go back to their homes to fight these battles without a lot of support.

The courage I saw in those kids and the support they gave one another was heartwarming as well as inspirational. Even though every week it was possible that half the group was using because of relapses or lack of commitment, they still had the courage to come to the group and face the confrontation of their peers and be forced to honestly look at how they really were doing. The life-or-death battle these kids fought one day at a time for their sobriety and some sense of normalcy in their lives touched me deeply and has forever been imprinted in my mind. These thirteen to eighteen year old kids had dealt with more adversity and trauma than I could have imagined. They all had courage, but only those who could combine honesty with themselves and a willingness to give up control over their lives had a chance of remaining sober. Many of the kids I had in group didn't make it. They started using again and often got in more trouble with the law and eventually dropped out of school. Others put on a real con, and many times fooled a lot of people, including me. In the end, they were only conning themselves. Still, other kids never really believed they had a problem and after a brief trial, dropped out of the group. But these kids remained loyal to one another and would usually support one another's sobriety, even if they could not maintain it themselves. One young man came to the group for over two years and was positive and supportive of all group members. He never put anyone down for slipping but always encouraged them to try again. He spoke to student organizations about the danger of drinking and using drugs. He was very active in the Fellowship of Christian Athletes organization. We were all shocked when two months before his graduation, he admitted to secretly drinking by himself from his father's keg in the basement. He was being admitted to a treatment center and wanted our support. The first feeling I felt was a sense of betrayal and then anger at his dishonesty. Then I realized the courage and loyalty it took for him to continue to positively support sobriety when he couldn't maintain it himself. He wasn't being hypocritical but rather wanted to help others to not make the same mistake he was making. He finally had reached his limit and gave up trying to control his life and sought help. Happily, he found sobriety, and though it is still one day at a time for him, he continues to be positive force for others in their struggle for sobriety.

Loyalty, honesty, and courage were the key traits of many of the group members, and they also shared intense moments, tender moments, and humorous moments with us all. As an adult who cared for them, I experienced the exhilaration and warmth of their successes and the heartache and pain of their failures. I never doubted their courage or their intent. It's a group of kids I will never forget, and the lessons they taught me will remain forever. I always try to remember not to be critical of others until I have walked in their shoes, and having done that, I marvel at their accomplishments rather than condemning their mistakes.

Thankfully, not all the lessons I've learned from kids have had the same intensity level as did the drug-alcohol support group, but the lessons I've learned from kids in other situations are just as important in the understanding of kids and their needs. Through my work in the schools as well as my private practice as a therapist, I have learned all kids need to "win" or to experience "success" in some aspects of their lives. The constant failures and unsuccessful endeavors will sink their self-esteem to such low levels that the only coping mechanisms they can turn to are unhealthy or even destructive.

When I started working in the schools, I had very little training in play therapy or any other successful methods of dealing with young children. A deck of UNO cards and a container of colored markers became the tools of my trade in working with younger children. It didn't take me long to realize, even in a brief period of fifteen- to twenty-minute sessions with my kids, something special was happening that helped form a strong and lasting relationship. There were no twenty questions or probing therapy techniques, for I found, in my limited time with kids, it was imperative to establish a trusting relationship while providing some boost to their self-esteem. This no-demand, no-expectation approach allowed them to relax, and the drawing or game-playing soon put a smile on their faces, giving them some respite from a day often filled with failure and social put-downs. I soon realized the fifteen to twenty minutes we spent together might have been the only time during their day they felt success. They could perform without pressure or feel overwhelmed by the expectations of others. My approach of complete acceptance and unconditional caring turned a simple game or drawing into a positive experience that was the beginning of a trusting relationship with an adult. For a while, I doubted whether a few minutes a week playing games with kids could really be of long-lasting significance. They soon taught me a moment of success or a time of positive reinforcement could, indeed, be a catalyst toward regaining a sense of confidence. In the twenty-five years I spent as a school social worker, I can't remember when this simple technique did not bring a smile to a kid's face and a sense of accomplishment in a world filled with discouragement. I also need to mention that my self-esteem has survived losing about 99 percent of all games with my kids. Often, when a child's self-esteem had increased, they became concerned with my feelings over not winning. I assured them they needed to win more than I did.

Seeing kids in the school ran the risk of even further damage to their self- esteem. If other kids put them down or made fun of them for seeing me, it could make things worse. One of the side benefits of playing games or doing fun things with them was it gave them something to tell the other children when they asked what they were doing with me. Instead of saying we were talking about their problems, they could say we were playing Uno and they won. This certainly had its drawbacks with some teachers, but through the years, they too have learned the lesson these kids needed a time to feel good about themselves and to have a chance to succeed. Oftentimes teachers too found the value of using drawing or things the kids feel good about as rewards and incentives for working hard on their schoolwork. With most of these kids, it was not their lack of ability to do the work but rather their lack of confidence in their ability. When we would build that confidence in one area, it often could be transferred to the academic areas as well. What kids tell us is there must be a payoff for their efforts, and that payoff is success.

All kids have unique gifts and talents, and the kids I worked with were not exceptions to that rule. Each one of the kids I have worked with is a special human being, regardless of their disability, whether physical, developmental, mental, or behavioral. These kids have so much to offer the world around them, but often they do not have a clue about their talents and abilities. I found those special traits must be drawn out of them. By the time I would see them, they would be discouraged, angry, confused, and they feel incapable of doing even the simplest of things. My responsibility and the responsibility of all those who worked with them was to get beyond their current behavior, attitudes, or academic achievement. There is a time to throw out intelligence tests, behavior rating scales, and self-concept measurement and to forget all those things the kids can't or won't do. We need to concentrate on what they can do and what their strengths and positive traits are. What these kids need is a reason for achievement and a method to their learning that makes sense to them. They need encouragement and a sense of belonging. That is why a simple approach of caring and acceptance can be the beginning of an emerging personality that can be pleasing to adults and can be acceptable for them as well. A key to unlocking these talents can allow them to teach others and to participate in a way that acknowledges their self-worth. I have encouraged these children to teach me their many talents and skills and to allow them to experience that sense of having something to offer someone else. The rest of this chapter will give examples of the many lessons I have learned from kids.

One of the young men I had worked with was a freshman in high school, and because of a smart mouth, he often spent much of the day in detention or in school suspension. This made it quite easy for me to see him because I did not have to take him from a class.

He had moved several times in his life and had currently been sent to live with his father on the farm because his mother could not handle him. This kid was a typical "throwaway" kid who nobody seemed to want. His self-concept was low, and his identity was that of a behavior problem. Who the kid "really" was defied the image he was maintaining. He was bright, sensitive, and had a terrific sense of humor. He loved farming and knew a great deal about all aspects of it. Like most of the kids I have worked with, I asked him to tell me some things he did well. One of those things was the game of cribbage. Ordinarily, I would not have enough time with him to learn a game like cribbage, but because of his usual time away from class, we had plenty of time. It turned out he was an excellent cribbage player and an even better teacher. He had patience and an effective way with words to describe the intricacies of the game. When the high school principal learned of our cribbage games, he was not pleased. He could not understand how playing a game could help this kid's behavior. After several discussions and a few cribbage games of his own, the principal understood that learning a kid's strength and using those strengths could, indeed, help with his behavior. By establishing relationships and having people advocate for him, the boy eventually became active in Future Farmers of America, took part in speech contests, and showed much improvement in not only his behavior but also his academics. I learned more than a cribbage game from him. I learned once again the importance of acknowledging a person's values and gifts.

Another instance of learning from my kids came from a self-contained classroom for kids with behavior disorders. These kids all had a history of failure in the classroom, and after trying many different motivational techniques for several months, the teacher learned the only way he could effectively instruct these kids was to help them feel good about themselves. This teacher decided to look outside the box. Some of the projects they became involved in included painting, putting together models, making and flying kites, being part of an archery team, and planning meets. They had an opportunity to show their abilities and to teach skills they were good at, like fishing and camping. I spent considerable time with this group, as many of them were on my caseload. My best work with these kids was when I became their student and had them teach me their skills. Also, because I wasn't very skilled in many of these areas, I was the perfect candidate for their sharing and teaching. I'll never forget the difference it made in our relationship when they knew they could teach me how to fish, how to use a bow safely, how to dig a hole in the ice to fish, how to pitch a tent, and how to cook a meal over an open fire. I have found it is much easier to convince kids they can learn in school when you value their knowledge and ability in other areas. Being needed and wanted was often uncommon for these kids, and the spark it ignited within them and their families was amazing.

I learned another very important lesson from a young lady who was a sophomore in high school and who was having a very difficult time with her classes. She also had trouble with her social interactions. Although her

English grade was a "D," she had a remarkable way with words when put into poetry. Although her spelling was atrocious and her grammar very poor, her content was magnificent. It showed a combination of sensitivity, insight, knowledge, compassion, and wisdom far beyond her age. She had a rhyme and rhythm to her poetry that kept your attention and a beauty and depth of meaning that touched my heart. I was so impressed with her work that I asked her if she had given it to the English teacher or had it published in the school paper. She acted really surprised and said, "No one has ever read these before."

She was totally unaware of the extent of her talent. She wrote because she felt her life very deeply and needed to express some of those feelings. She once again taught me to never judge a book by its cover, or in this case, don't judge a sensitive young lady by her academic output. Once the English teacher and the school paper advisors were told about her abilities and shown her work, her deficiencies in spelling and grammar were no longer deemed that important, and they became strong advocates for her. They began to nurture her for her innate talent and inner being. How many gifted and talented kids do we miss because we fail to seek their abilities and focus only on what they can't do?

I met one very special girl when she was in eighth grade and having a difficult time. She had a disorder called Tourette's syndrome, and it caused her body and face to twitch and contort without her having control over it. With Tourette's, the more upset you become, the more the symptoms are exacerbated. She had become so devastated by the time I was asked to see her that her parents were considering taking her out of school. She was ashamed and embarrassed by her twitching, and she had been teased quite badly by her peers. After getting to know her, I found her to be a bright, sensitive young lady who could describe her symptoms and her feelings about her situation. She had a good understanding of what Tourette's was and how it affected people physically and socially. When I praised her for being able to teach me about her disorder, she was overwhelmed with the idea that she could teach someone else. This young lady, together with the middle school staff and her parents, decided the best way to help her socially was to make the other students aware of her disorder. A film was shown to all the other students, and this seemed to have a positive effect on how she was treated. Then she did a very courageous thing: She wrote a paper about Tourette's and then turned it into a report she gave to her class. When she was able to teach others and to talk freely with them about her disorder, she became less self-conscious, and her symptoms became minimal. She not only taught me courage but also reaffirmed the value of being able to teach and share your expertise with others. This young lady went on to high school and did well academically and socially. She also was able to work for a local supermarket and was able to deal with the public without any noticeable problems.

I think the most important lesson I have learned from kids is even one person who cares can make a difference in a child's life. One person who recognizes their strength and abilities can nurture and advocate for the child. Sometimes we don't even notice what a difference we make, but I assure you, we do. It may be an act of kindness, a thoughtful comment, a small present, or the gift of time. They may seem like trivial things, but they can change the direction of a child's life. Having someone to care, to notice them, to treat them special, to acknowledge their self-worth, someone who allows them to help or teach other kids, that person can be any of us who are in that child's life. Never, ever, think your time with kids is wasted, for if given sincerely, it can make a difference in their lives. If you have listened and heard what they have to say, or if you have given a gentle touch of your hand or a warm smile, you may have been the key that unlocked a seemingly unreachable goal for a child. You may have been the one person to be kind to this child in their whole day, and it may have turned that day around. Never think what we do for kids out of love doesn't have an impact. Hundreds of kids throughout the years have shown me what seems to be such a small amount of time or kindness can have a tremendous and meaningful effect on the heart of a child.

Chapter Four
Study and Discussion Guide

1. Talk about the importance of kids teaching adults about areas in which they have special skills.
2. Why could something as simple as teaching an adult how to play cribbage be helpful in their relationship?
3. Discuss the importance of understanding the feelings kids go through when they become involved in drugs and alcohol as a means of coping with the difficulties in their lives.
4. When a kid can teach others about her disability, explain the sense of freedom and pride that can come from it.
5. Try to realize how many things our kids and students teach us about life when we are working with them.

FIVE

Life Skills: The Longer I Live, The More Kids Teach Me About the Meaning of Life

In the years I worked as a counselor for Lutheran Social Services, I had the opportunity to work with youth who were having emotional and behavioral problems within their families and communities. I quickly learned their emotional state affected their entire lives. They needed caring and nurturing for them to feel like worthwhile human beings. Not only did their immediate feelings need to be dealt with, but we also needed to understand their environment and the people who had the most impact on them. When I started working as a school social worker, I quickly realized, within the academic setting, there were certain expectations of children, regardless of their family and or emotional circumstances. These expectations were often not realistic for some of these kids. At times these kids were far too overwhelmed with their lives to be able to handle the stresses of academic learning. In the words of an old saying, "When you are up to your knees in alligators, you forget that your mission was to drain the swamp." When kids are "up to their ears in emotional problems," they too forget the mission of learning in school. A lesson kids today have taught and continue to teach all of us in education is, until we deal with the person and their hurts, their pain, and their physical and emotional problems, we cannot begin to open the door to their learning. When a child has not eaten breakfast, is chilled to the bone from lack of proper clothing, is upset because of a fight before leaving for school, or has the fear a parent might not be there when they return, then reading, writing, and arithmetic do not seem very important to them. When school responds to the individual needs of each of these kids, it is remarkable what we can learn about life and living from them.

School breakfasts, providing of winter clothes, individual or group counseling, breakfast clubs, peer counseling, sharing time, guidance classes, and many other innovative programs within the schools are tiny steps in addressing the needs of our kids, other than through academics. Our schools have come to realize we live in a different world than we did twenty years ago, and kids come to us with many different and varied needs. Rather than viewing them only as academic students to be taught a structured curriculum, we also need to address their other needs.

This chapter will look at the many lessons of life my kids have taught me and the need to remember that kids often have as much to teach us as we do them.

One of the most important lessons kids can teach us about life is the value of the family. Of course, we would all agree how important the family is. What we need to remember is the perspective of the child. We cannot judge the family based on our values or standards of living. Even though we may see a child as lacking in some areas and feel the family is not providing the necessary elements for the child's success, it doesn't mean there isn't a tremendous sense of loyalty and love in the family. Sometimes the best intentions of school personnel can create a tremendous distance between the school and home. An intended act of kindness that is misunderstood by the family can be perceived by the family as either meddling or putting them down. We must be careful not to over analyze or judge families without learning more about their situation. A little extra time and consideration for the families' feelings can help us give them the benefit of doubt. This can often be the difference between having a working relationship and an oppositional one with the family. Lack of knowledge, underdeveloped parenting skills, and financial difficulties can be interpreted as neglect or lack of caring on the parents' part. Before we jump to conclusions, we need to visit the family and put ourselves in their shoes. We are often amazed at the genuine concern and willingness to help on the part of the parents when we had assumed they did not care. When kids give us the message that their family is important to them, we need to listen and acknowledge their feelings. One of the benefits of my job was I would often get to visit the families of the kids I worked with, and usually, it was in their homes. You can learn a lot more about a family when you meet them in their comfort zone. They also are much more willing to let you into their hearts and minds. Visiting the family in their homes allowed me to see them relaxed and interacting in their normal way. Oftentimes families are intimidated and defensive when they come to school to meet with the teachers and other staff. Being in the homes of my kids' families deepened my understanding of the importance of their families to them.

When I came as an advocate for the family and had already been accepted by their child, they often let down their guard and showed the love and care that exist among the family members. I didn't look for good housekeeping or a house in good repair or for academic tools, such as computers or individual study areas for the children; instead, I looked for and most often would find the feeling of love within the family. That's what gave me the basis for advocating for the family in the school setting. It also gave me inroads for suggesting changes within the family that would benefit the child. If we would only come to judge or to expect confrontation from families, then we would usually get what we expected. If, instead, we acknowledge the importance of a child's family to them, we often can be of benefit to the family and the child as well.

Another important lesson I have learn about life from my kids is kids need to be allowed to be kids. We have too many parents who have allowed their children to grow up way too fast. Some even encourage them to become the parental child, letting them take over some of the duties and responsibilities of the parent. All too often we see fifth- and sixth-grade kids who are responsible for two or three younger siblings in the mornings and after school as well. There are children of all ages who try to protect and care for their mother or father in divorce situations or alcoholic homes or abusive families, where the child will try to protect their parent from an abusive spouse. These kids are quickly losing their childhood and are not allowed to just be kids. When they try to act their age among peers, they are often considered immature or inappropriate, and at times they do not know how to properly interact with their peers.

One of my friends was a guidance counselor when I worked with him. He also was studying to be a play therapist and now is certified and working in his field. A wonderful thing I learned from him was how to allow kids to be kids. In our groups together, we taught kids to just be themselves and to be kids in appropriate and acceptable ways. We used group settings in seeing kids, and it allowed time for kids to teach one another and learn from one another. Oftentimes the kids who had the most difficulty were allowed to pick the other children for their group. This gave them a sense of power and control. These were usually kids who had very little control in their lives, and with a sense of control came a sense of trust and security. Often this is what they needed for them to let down their guard and be a kid within the group.

Kids who have been treated as young adults need the freedom and the guidance to learn how to be kids again. It was amazing the differences we could see in kids after they learn it's OK to just be a kid. Unfortunately, many of the kids who have difficult family situations have trouble in school as well and feel they can never live up to anyone's expectations. The weight of the world is literally upon many of these kids. Being able to relax and enjoy being a kid was not that easy either at home or at school. When they feel safe just being kids, they reaffirm the lesson we need to learn: Kids just need to be kids.

At times, when kids get into middle school and high school, academic expectations increase, and kids often are not allowed opportunities to just be kids. The pressure and emphasis from middle school on up is for kids to be grown-up and mature and to truly act as little adults. What we, educators, need to remember is these kids too have the need to be kids. If you've had much contact with middle school kids, you know there is often a major conflict within these kids between being grown-up and being kids. Unfortunately, as adults, we never know which person will show up, the adult or the kid. There needs to be activities for these kids that allow for some silliness and nurture their continued need for laughter and fun. Many teachers build in times for games and activities that allow them to let down their guard and just be kids. For them to grow into responsible yet happy adults, they need to keep that fun-loving side to them. Likewise, high school students also need to remember how to have fun. They need that kid within to remain part of their lives. It is important they learn they can let their hair down, be silly and funny without having to use drugs or alcohol. Church youth groups, community theatre, FFA, 4H, and other organizations often utilize humor and games to help allow these young adults still be kids. Life is serious enough for young people without denying their inner child and their need to have fun and just be a kid.

Kids are often not given credit for their sensitivity and depth of feeling. A lesson kids have taught me is their incredible capacity for compassion and sensitivity and abstract-thinking. Sometimes we write kids off as not being able to think of anyone but themselves. The developmental stages of life often have kids self-centered in the normal development of their personality. In reality, kids often have a strong sense of interest and concern for others. Many of the examples of kindness and caring and concern I have experienced have come from kids, who usually have their plates full of their concerns. Instead of having tunnel vision and only thinking of themselves, they have concern and compassion for others that helps them in dealing with their problems.

One young man I worked with was certified with a behavior disorder and certainly worked hard to live up to that label. He was often disruptive in class, would get into fights, use obscene language, and do things that border-lined on vandalism. Yet through all these attempts to live up to his reputation, he was the one person in his class who had the courage and compassion to tell the teachers when his classmates were considering suicide or hurting themselves or others. He cared enough about others to try to help them, even though he was having difficulty with his emotions and behavior. He also showed kindness and caring to younger children and would often help them with homework or other activities they were involved in. His actions toward others in times of crisis belied his perceived lack of concern for himself that was often displayed at school or home. It's too bad kids like him cannot transfer more of that care and concern they have for others to themselves.

Another young lady, who at the time was in eighth grade, seems to spend her whole day making others around her miserable. As a student with attention deficit disorder, she chose not to take medication. She became very oppositional, especially toward any authority figure at school and to her parents at home. She painted herself into a corner she could not escape from. Yet this same girl had extraordinary patience with her multi-handicapped sister and seemed very pleasant and easy to be around while she was helping her sister. In trying to help her change her attitude, she was given the opportunity to work with kids in the area education preschool in her building. She had a gentle touch with children who had special needs. It brought a tenderness and kindness in her personality not usually seen at school or at home. She was also chosen to be a "bus buddy" for another child with special needs, and that all but eliminated her trouble with peers and the bus driver. What she needed was a sense of belonging and being needed. She had built up her nasty disposition as a defense mechanism to cover up her hurts and pain. Her sensitivity toward others in need showed she had a special insight into the feelings and pain of others because of all she had experienced herself. Her problems did not quickly melt away, but in the years to come, she eventually went back to school to become a nurse. She also became a mother, and this too brought out her care. Eventually, she joined a Christian outreach group that did mission work overseas, and she has continued to grow and flourish.

Another young man with a certified behavior disorder (you might be sensing a pattern here) many times amazed me with his sensitivity and compassion for others. The tenderness and kindness he had shown toward those special teachers and aides who had worked closely with him shows how a little time and love can bring the best out of kids who struggle with authority and relationship in general. Many years ago this boy came up to me on the first day of school, and I knew he really needed to tell me something. This was about a month after my daughter had been in a tragic accident, and she was left with multiple injuries, physical and emotional. He told me he heard about the accident on the radio and had been thinking of my daughter and me and was praying for both of us. He said he would have sent me a card, but he didn't know my address. With tears streaming down my cheeks, I gave this boy a hug, remembering how many people have written him and his family off years ago. How far had this boy come despite the many obstacles at home and at school. When he had a chance to be helpful and caring to others, he could then have a sense of value and belonging as well.

Many years ago I was chosen by my peers to be school social worker of the year. This certainly was an award that deeply touched my heart. But what made it even better was reading the letters of support from all my schools and coworkers. Even after I received the state reward, I received many letters and e-mails of congratulations. One of these will always stand out in my mind. A young friend I had worked with for several years sent me the following card of congratulations. His message was simple: "You deserve the award. You helped me a lot, I miss you and I love you."

This young man has childhood autism. School and life had been a struggle for him. He graduated from high school in a special program and has continued to struggle as a young adult. I just wish everyone could see his strengths and love as I did. For me to receive that kind of caring message from him was a far greater reward than I could ever expect. Kids, no matter what their disability may be, can think deeply and reach outside of themselves to touch others.

Another lesson I have learned about life from kids is to never underestimate the ability or the desire or the determination of a kid. Our schools are filled with underachieving kids. These are kids who have given up on themselves and who others have also given up on. We have bright kids who suffer from low self- esteem, lack of confidence, and a sense of hopelessness toward school. Many of these kids are in programs where the expectations for these children are much lower than their abilities would justify. Their performance in these programs becomes even lower than these reduced expectations. We also have other kids with limited abilities who have suffered from too high expectations and, again, are now performing even lower than what would be considered reasonable for their abilities. This is not meant to be a negative view of our schools, only a realistic assessment that we still have a long way to go. We need to continue to teach each child according to their needs. We also need to catch these problems before they negatively affect their self-esteem. We also need to reach our kids who have learning disabilities, mild mental disorders, childhood autism, those related disorders along the pervasive disorder spectrum, attention deficit disorder, Tourette's syndrome, and all other disabilities that affect our kids. We need to learn to recognize their strengths and abilities and design programs that specifically deal with their learning capabilities so they can believe in themselves and keep their self-esteem. When that is in place, then these children can achieve far beyond our original expectations. The key is encouragement, nurturing, and helping them achieve success. If we can blend these three ingredients into each one of their individualized education plans, then we will be amazed at the results. Many of our innovative, creative, and caring teachers within the many school districts I have served have seen these positive results when the child's strengths are recognized and encouraged. We all need to continue in our efforts to educate not only our teachers but also our parents and other professionals in our education systems. We need to make them more aware of the different learning styles of children and ways to build up kids and to encourage and work with them when difficulties occur. We can greatly reduce the number of unhappy or underachieving kids if we treat each one just as they are. Each one is an individual with unique abilities and needs.

I remember working with a student who was having tremendous difficulties with academics and social skills. He was in second grade when I started working with him. His family took him to the doctor in fifth grade, when he was diagnosed with attention deficit disorder with hyperactivity. He was started on medication agreed upon by the doctor and family as well as this boy. At that time the boy was discouraged and lacking in self-esteem and confidence, often underachieving according to his abilities. During the next three years, from fifth grade to eighth, a very significant change occurred. With the help of his doctors, his parents, his teachers, and his counselors, he became more successful in the classroom, and with his peers and with his determination, he went from being a student who received many Ds and Fs to making the honor roll for the first time ever during the first semester of his eighth-grade year. From being a child with very little social ability, he became active socially and well liked. He was elected to the student council, something none of us could have imagined during his struggles. The change occurred because those closest to him refused to underestimate his abilities. They also refused to accept anything less than his best effort from him. Once he believed in himself, his determination and desire took over. From a child at high risk for failure, he became a normal, happy teenager, who then achieved up to his ability level. This is what can happen when teachers, parents, and all involved with a student work together and believe in their ability and heart.

I have seen many children with learning disabilities and attention deficit disorder make terrific progress with their academics and with their social skills. But this happens only after these kids have received the kinds of assistance they have needed. The assistance could be special programming through an educational resource room. It also can happen after the child has received medication for the ADHD or has structured behavior management programs for the school and home to help them in dealing with organizational skills. When we could address their difficulty with a positive approach, we could improve how they saw themselves and give them a taste of success. Then we were often pleasantly surprised by the enormous growth we could see.

A fourth-grade boy I worked with for about a year was very interesting. He was very bright but had difficulties focusing in the classroom. He became bored quite easily and at times could be disruptive in the class. Although he had potential to be a leader, he was being seen as a negative influence. We had many conferences with the parents and attempted behavior modification without a great deal of success. His parents and his teachers became frustrated. Finally, they agreed an evaluation for ADD could give them some answers. The parents then agreed to medication. The difference with him was immediate and astounding. He now was able to focus in the classroom, and his academic potential was soon achieved. Socially, he became a positive leader with his peers, and he became a role model for some of his friends who have behavior problems. He was a determined young man but had become discouraged by his lack of success. Thanks to his parents and teachers working with him, he was able to live up to his potential, academically and socially.

These are just a couple of examples of what happens when we look at the child's strength and then work together to nurture our kids. We must never underestimate a kid's ability.

Another lesson of life I've learned from kids is to never, ever, give up on anyone. Many times I've worked with kids who seem to have given up on themselves, and the system they live in seems to have given up on them as well. I have learned, no matter how angry or depressed or lethargic or discouraged a kid may be, they need someone in their lives who refuses to give up on them. Be it a teacher, a counselor, a friend, or a parent, kids need to know someone will continue to believe in them and care for them and pray for them, even when they have given up on themselves. The result of not giving up on them can often be the difference in getting a child to believe in themselves as well. Time and again, I have seen the faith of one or two people make a miraculous difference in the life of a child. Some of the kids I thought had little chance to turn their lives around have done so because someone they cared about refused to give up on them. I've seen kids with behavior disorders change their behavior and adjust back to regular classes. I've seen learning-disabled children rise above the expectations and not only go to college but also be successful there. I've seen children with autism learn to cope with the social world around them. I've seen kids with Tourette's syndrome teach others about their condition and be able to handle their symptoms and walk proudly with their peers. I've seen children with ADHD use their talents and abilities, despite their additional difficulties. With all these kids, there has been a common ingredient to their successes; that ingredient is someone important in their lives refused to give up on them when their situations seemed very difficult and their success seemed improbable.

It is heartwarming for me to look back at the many lessons of life my kids have taught me. I also realize the longer I live, the more kids will continue to teach me about life. Kids have so many gifts to share with us, if we will only open our hearts and minds and souls to what they are trying to teach us.

Chapter Five
Study and Discussion Guide

1. What programs in our schools deal with meeting the needs of our kids outside the realm of academics?

2. Tell me about the loyalty kids have for their families, regardless of their living situation.

3. How can good intentions of teachers sometimes cause more harm than good?

4. In what way do parents' predetermined attitudes toward the school affect the performance of their children?

5. Families can be important advocates for their children. Describe how this can happen so their input can be valuable.

The Wonderful World of Work

Kids often have very different views of work, and they can change as they get older and become more experienced. Some kids learn a work ethic at a very early age, by doing chores, while others have very little work experience until they are in high school and want to earn money for their social lives or possibly for a car. It's interesting to contrast kids' views toward working for money and working at home or school. Some parents can project the view to their kids that school is their job and to encourage and expect their kids to treat schoolwork with the same effort and respect that would be expected from employers. Others put more value on the working world than school, and that is often reflected in the downslide of performance once a job is found. There needs to be a middle ground where value is seen in all the responsibilities kids have, whether in school, in extracurricular activities, with the chores at home, or at the jobsite.

Work, whether in school or at home, must be seen as having some value by the child. This needs to start at a young age and be done with careful consideration for the child's self-esteem. Most jobs are not going to be done as well by a child as they would by either a parent or teacher. Adults must be careful not to discourage the child by expecting perfection. We need to give patient and clear instructions and allow your child to do the best they can.

In school, teachers can be very helpful to kids by allowing them to be leaders in different classroom activities and encouraging them in different tasks they are helping with. Little things like getting the milk, being line leaders, erasing boards, taking attendance, helping collect lunch tickets, and other nonacademic tasks can help all students experience success and receive praise for their efforts This can help all kids, especially those who are not having success academically. It encourages responsibility and leadership while giving them some of the skills they need in attempting and completing a job. If kids are given a chance to be helpers and to have nonacademic success, it is much easier to get them give effort in academic areas, even when they have difficulties in those areas. It also helps teachers and other adults be more willing to give kids the extra modifications and help they need to be successful in academics. It also will be giving them credibility with other kids because of their understanding and faith in them in the nonacademic areas. These prework activities can help prepare kids for the work ethic necessary to succeed in school, sports, and work in the future.

At home, how the parents introduce work through chores or duties can have a lasting effect on how kids view work later. The tasks or chores need to be divided fairly for the kids and delegated according to their skills and abilities when possible. The parent needs to be patient, exhibiting understanding in their expectations in the performance of chores and not to expect perfection from young children. They also need to praise their efforts and offer constructive criticism in gentle ways. Kids' willingness to take on responsibility and accept the pressures of real job situations often depends on how their initial work experience impacts them.

The actual work experience is different for each kid, but how they handle it depends on their prework experiences. The kid who gets discouraged easy on tasks at home and school is very vulnerable to not sticking it out in their first work experience. The kid who is late or often absent at school can likewise have difficulties with attendance and promptness on their first job. The kid who has learned the importance of hard work and the need for promptness often starts well in their first job experience. So it is important to remember that the prework experience we give kids can help their performance in actual work situations. Many of our high schools have programs of work experience for kids that are at risk in their work skills.

This program gave them supervised experience and coaches them in the jobsite and social skills needed there.

Kids view work quite differently as well. Some seeing it only as a temporary means to an end or, in other words, money for their present needs. Others perceive it as the beginning of a career. Still others see it as valuable experience for more important jobs in the future. For some kids, work is a welcome opportunity that gives them more positive feedback than what they perceive the school does. For some kids, work complicate their lives by making them divide time among school, home, and social priorities and can become overwhelming for them. Others use work as a way of spending time and see it more as a social outlet for them. For some kids, it is a source of self-esteem they are not receiving from home or school. Although the reasons are often different, the importance of how they perform and how that affects their lives is very real. Some kids become job-hoppers, quitting or getting fired from many different jobs without thinking about how that can affect future employment. Others quit when they get mad or upset, never thinking it might be difficult finding their next job. I would always tell kids not to quit one job until they already have another job waiting for them. Then they should do it with grace, giving proper notice and gratitude for the job they are leaving.

I have seen where a good work experience can eventually be a catalyst for improved school behavior and performance. A few years ago, in one of the high schools I worked at, a high school junior was giving academic teachers fits with his disruptions in the classroom, general surliness of attitude, and refusals to accept corrections or criticism. This young man was negative to his teachers and some peers and would not accept either help or discipline from the administrative or counseling staffs. This same kid worked at a local grocery store and had a completely different attitude and overall personality difference between the two settings. His attitude at work was positive; he was courteous and friendly with his coworkers and to the customers. He had no trouble following rules or directions. His bosses and coworkers were very positive about him and could see him becoming a permanent employee. Thanks to the cooperation with his employers, we were able to set up a program that could work for him at school. He was set up on a contract that did not allow second chances in his classroom for behavior problems. One negative outburst or refusal to follow directions and he was out of the class for the day and received a zero as well. The expectations for his attendance, promptness, and attitude expected at school were increased, and he was no longer given the benefit of the doubt. His employer further helped the situation by agreeing to not have him work on the days he was not displaying appropriate behavior at school. What happened was exciting. Rather than becoming more belligerent or rebellious when the expectations were increased and the structure became stronger, he instead became more compliant and eventually started showing an improved attitude in classes. The instances of being sent out of the classroom decreased until it didn't happen at all. His grades and attendance improved dramatically. He found out feeling good about himself didn't have to be an either work or school alternative but could be in both settings. In this case, the world of work helped his world of school become more acceptable to him.

Another girl I worked with was having many difficulties at home and at school, but work seemed to be her one place where she felt good about herself. She got behind on her schoolwork and started being tardy for classes and sometimes missing school completely, which got her further behind and became more discouraging for her. Even with her school difficulties, she continued to always go to work on time and show good work habits and social skills on the job. The contrast between the two settings helped the school look at the need to make her academic setting more successful for her so she could feel as comfortable there as she did at work. After additional testing, it was discovered she had a severe learning disability, and the expectations had been too high for her, causing frustration and discouragement. When we learned of her success at work, we started changing her school programming and setting her up for success at school also. It wasn't long before attendance and promptness improved at school and her overall self-esteem received reinforcement at both settings.

Some kids get involved in the work world without knowing the additional time and stress it can involve. If the employer doesn't take into consideration that the kid is still in school, excess time expectations can lead to serious difficulties with academics and put the kid in the difficult struggle between the importance of work and the emphasis on school. Parents and teachers often don't realize the hours being expected of the kid and just become critical when the schoolwork starts to decline. These same employees often have kids working late shifts that interfere with the kids' need for sleep, and hence, tardiness, absences, or lethargy results in school. When we understand that kids are still kids, whether they can do adult jobs or not, we can help them set limits for them at work. Sometimes the school or parents need to intervene at the workplace to let them know the negative effect of the job on their schoolwork. The self-esteem from working as well as the money often puts the kids in a difficult struggle for loyalty to job, home, and school. As much as the kids want to be responsible adults, there are times that limits still need to be set for them, and workplace restrictions can be one of those limits that are difficult for them to establish by themselves.

The world of work can be a good way for kids to experiment with their interests and try jobs that look appealing to them. This can help them determine what types of jobs they would like to have later in life. A girl who is thinking of being a nurse may volunteer in a hospital or become a nurse's aide to get a feel for the profession she is considering. This kind of experimentation can help her find out where her interests lie before she spends a great deal of time going to school for a profession she really won't enjoy. My youngest daughter went to work at the same pizza parlor her sister worked at. She found out quickly making pizzas and waiting tables were not her thing. To some, there may be no need to have a connection between early jobs and their eventual careers, and a means to their end is simply making some money while in high school.

Some kids have had little responsibilities at home and have not learned the skills needed for work. Two brothers I worked with came out to my acreage to work off $50 for an old car I was letting them have. Working on a farm was not what they were used to doing. The elder brother started right in shoveling manure out of my riding arena, while the younger brother was sweeping out my stable area. The younger brother was supposed to finish sweeping and then help his brother in the stable area. Every time I checked on him, he was playing with my cats or looking at my saddles or resting. I will say my stables were swept clean, but it was obvious he was not planning on shoveling manure. They were well-mannered boys whom I had become close to, but doing chores was not something they were used to doing. Later they enjoyed riding my horses, but I don't think farmwork is going to be high on their career list.

The world of work for kids is one of learning and making mistakes and preparing themselves for later in life. It is a way of socializing and of making money, and it often gives them a sense of self- esteem they don't get from other areas of their lives. As parents and teachers, we can help the learning experience for kids by giving them small and manageable tasks they can be successful with early on in their lives. We can build up their skills and their confidence to prepare them with the work skills they will need later.

Chapter Six
Study and Discussion Guide

1. Name several things parents can do at home to prepare our kids for work.

2. Describe the importance of a good work ethic for kids beginning in the working world.

3. There are many interest inventories that can be used to identify what kids would like to do in their work. How are these helpful in making job placements within the realm of the school?

4. Kids can have different motivations for working. Name some of their reasons for wanting to work.

5. Define the difference between a job and a career.

6. When kids fail or quit their first job, what effect can that have on future employment?

SEVEN

Every Day Working with Kids Is Seasoned with the Spice of Their Humor

This chapter is a difficult one to write simply because there is so much humor in working with kids, it's hard to know where to start. I was struggling through the first draft. I finally felt fairly satisfied with the content when I shut off the computer without pressing the "save box," and whoosh, my chapter on humor was history. I later was lamenting to my daughter that perhaps this was a divine intervention, and He was not pleased with my content. She looked me straight in the eye and said, "Dad, don't blame God for your problem."

I'm sure there is some humor in this situation; I just haven't found it yet. I had to begin anew looking at the tremendous gift of humor I found every day I worked with kids in the school system. There were certainly times in my other positions as a therapist when I found humorous situations with the kids I worked with, but it was nothing like the fertile ground provided by the school setting and the many different situations that lend themselves to humor. Granted, at the time some of these situations may not have seemed humorous to all involved, but they supplied me with a plentiful supply of smiles and chuckles throughout the day.

Kids of all ages, especially the younger ones, seem to have that special knack of saying and doing the unexpected and doing it in a humorous way. Whether it is kids interacting with one another or with adults, their innocence, honesty, and straightforwardness could create an atmosphere where humor abounds. We've all heard the saying, "Kids say the funniest things," but when you experience it every day, you know that statement was not exaggerated. If adults will just sit back and enjoy kids, letting down their walls and defenses, the joy derived from kids can be beyond description.

If we learn to laugh at ourselves as well as with the kids around us, we create a setting where humor is acceptable, contagious, and inevitable. We need to remember almost everything young children do, they are doing for the first time. Their awkwardness and wariness at attempting new tasks or interactions can often be very humorous. As adults, we need to be careful never to laugh at their attempts and to always encourage and reinforce their efforts while helping them learn to laugh at themselves and others when something humorous happens to them. The best way we, parents and teachers, can help them is by modeling this attitude ourselves and not overreacting when kids notice our mistakes or errors. It also helps when we can recognize and point out some of our faults and failures and to point them out in a humorous and lighthearted manner.

I've never thought of myself as an overly serious person, but neither have I considered myself as an overly humorous or cheerful person, but kids say they enjoy my laughter, smile, and cheerfulness. I think I am viewed that way because of the atmosphere and setting of dealing with kids daily. They bring out the best in me and have an incredible way of tickling my funny bone. I am sure my perceived cheerfulness is a reflection of what I see in the kids I work with, and I know it becomes easy to relax and smile and have fun with kids who have such a positive effect on who I am. I guess I have dealt with enough tragedy and hurt and pain that I savor those moments of laughter and happiness and try to model to my kids the need for humor and cheerfulness and the part it plays in helping us through the tougher times. It's the smiles, laughter, and playfulness of kids that helps me have the courage and sustaining power to deal with kids and families when stress, pain, unhappiness, and tragedy occur. If I did not recognize and enjoy the humor of kids daily, I'm not sure I could handle the more serious aspects of my job. Working in the schools allowed me that kind of balance many other positions in my field do not.

For the remainder of this chapter, I would like to share a variety of the humorous situations I have experienced in the twenty-four years I spent working with kids in the school setting. The tremendous relationships and caring teachers and counselors establish with their kids help them feel comfortable enough to be themselves and share who they are with others. Many of the situations I will share include colleagues of mine who cared enough about the kids they work with to laugh at themselves and with the kids in their care. They are genuine and caring in the atmosphere they have created for the kids they work with.

For many years, I used puppets with early elementary and preschool groups and have found many of my most humorous moments happening in these groups. The kids would always enjoy the puppets, and the use of puppets seemed to set the tone for not only humor, but also very open and genuine communications. Whether it was puppets from counseling programs, like Duso, Pumsey, Q-Bear, or the puppets I have accumulated over the years, they seem to add a unique component that lends itself to some hilarious moments.

One example was when I was going to introduce Ralph, my big brown fuzzy dog, to a preschool "listening skills class," my coworker suggested Ralph should have some clothes to wear and not be "naked." My wife agreed to make some puppet clothes and equipped Ralph with a hat, gloves, a vest, and some shoes, so he was ready to go. A few minutes into our introductory session, a four-year-old girl raised her hand and said, "Why is Ralph wearing clothes? Everyone knows that dogs don't wear clothes."

Well, almost everyone knew, but I guess we didn't, so much for Ralph's wardrobe.

Another time, when I was using Duso the Dolphin in a first-grade class, a rather disgruntled student informed me he could see my lips move when Duso was talking. Rather than have a discussion with a first-grader about the difference between a ventriloquist and an amateur puppeteer, I just smiled and said, "You're right, you can see my lips move when Duso talks, and that's OK. Like most things with young children, a simple and direct answer is all they need most of the time.

My good friend, Jerry Moss, was a counselor in one of my elementary schools, and we were doing a guidance class in his school. He was convinced the use of puppets in the Duso program were just not his thing. After teasing him I had a made-to-order adult Duso costume for him to wear, he was even more wary. The day to start the program was very interesting. By the end of the first class, there was Jerry, sitting on the floor with the kids, cheerfully singing the Duso song with a smile and glow only working with kids can give you. I had to smile and chuckle at the same time, as I watched this slightly rotund friend of mine swaying to the musical lyrics as he held the hands of the children nearest him. After the first class, we had numerous humorous and yet heartwarming sessions that included me dancing a "special dance" for all the kids amid many laughs and smiles. I had learned long before being yourself and at times acting silly and letting your hair down with kids is not only laughable, but also models for the kids that being a kid should be fun.

At one of the preschools, I was introducing my puppet Ralph to the class, along with my psychologist friend, and as is often the case, Ralph was being passed to each of the kids to hold and hug and feel his fur. Suddenly, one little boy reached up to my friend's full beard and while stroking it, said, "Ralph's fur is nice, but I like his fur better."

Many times during our groups that year and in the years to come some child would pay attention to his beard, and he always good-naturedly endured and enjoyed it. We found in those groups as in most groups of kids that laughter is contagious, and when something is funny, the result never needs to be embarrassment, defensiveness, or shyness but rather can fill the room with the giggling and laughter of little kids enjoying humor with one another.

Even though I have already indicated I am no ventriloquist and that the puppets are just that, puppets, I still had some funny incidents around my transporting and putting them away. One morning after I had finished with a puppet group, I was hurriedly putting Ralph and Sunny Bunny away, upside down. A little girl tugged at my sleeve and said, "Dave, you know you shouldn't put Ralph and Sunny Bunny upside down because they won't be able to breathe."

Another time with that same group, I was responding to why the puppets weren't with me, and I said I had left them in my car. A little boy said, "Dave, you know they shouldn't be left in a car by themselves. It's cold today, and they might freeze."

After that, I was more careful when I gave them an excuse for forgetting my puppets. What I have learned from these and other such occasions are, even though the puppets aren't real, they are interacting with the kids in a very real way, and the children expect them to be treated in the same way we treat one another—not a bad lesson for us all.

My puppets were used in a lot of different ways, in individual counseling and in groups. It certainly gave kids nonthreatening ways to communicate feelings. Humor is just one of the wonderful results of their use.

In addition to puppet groups, I also spent a lot of my time with small groups and special education classes doing social skills in which, as facilitators, we model appropriate behavior and used the time for teaching and practicing the various social skills. Again, because of the relationships we establish in these groups and our willingness to be genuine and honest, we often have situations filled with humor in the process.

One fall a new school psychologist was joining our middle school social skills group in a special education classroom. I had let him know these kids were straightforward, honest, and open. They also could be quite bold and curious. I obviously hadn't prepared him for what was to come. Shortly after our introduction, one young man looked at him and said, "What is that hole in your ear for?" He continued, "Did you wear earrings?"

The school psychologist stuttered and stammered and finally said the earring hole was healed over, and he didn't wear earrings. *And* he thought the subject was done. Instead, the boy proceeded to ask him what kind of earrings he wore and why did he decide to quit wearing them. Although it caught him off guard, he handled it very patiently and kindly and soon became a favorite with the kids. He quickly learned the value of his openness and genuineness in relating to the kids in the group, and it also made him more at ease for future groups. In the meantime, I was given a few smiles and chuckles during his initiation. He also learned at times it is more important to answer a kid's curiosity than it is to correct their social inappropriateness and that social skill learning comes with practice and role-modeling in a safe and secure environment.

Several years ago, I was teaching life skills in a special education classroom for fifth- and sixth-grade students, and our lesson was to learn to give and receive compliments. After the usual practice in class, I gave them an assignment to practice complimenting others during the week. From that time on, whenever I would enter the building, these kids would find me and compliment me on my shirt, my shoes, my tie, etc. Although awkward at the beginning, these students became proficient and comfortable giving compliments and eventually learned to compliment on a feeling level as well as a material level. In the meantime, other staff members gave me a rough time over setting these kids up to give me compliments. I just shrugged and replied, "You're just jealous because I thought of it first, and besides, we all need compliments once in a while."

When you teach children it's OK to make mistakes and not to be upset when corrected, you also need to be able to model that for them. Making silly little mistakes came naturally to me, so that was not a problem. I remember one time presenting to a class, when a boy told me my shoe was untied. I thanked him for telling me, and while I was leaning over to tie it, a little girl whispered to me, "It's all right, Mr. Hoye, I have trouble keeping my shoes tied too."

Often kids would let me know my coat was buttoned wrong, or my shirttail was out, or I had a label showing, or I had food on my mouth. But through it all, we had a few laughs, and they learned it was OK to make mistakes, and corrections come from love and not just from authority.

Some of the games I have kids play in groups lead themselves to laughter while helping kids develop confidence in themselves. It is also a place to let go of their shyness and self-consciousness. The facilitator must be willing to be the first one to model during the game. Whether it was Pictionary; charades; win, lose, and draw; or just some of the exercises I have created, I needed to, in all my silliness, act out the same things I expected them to do. One morning, when I was doing my best rendition of riding a horse, the principal came into the room, took one look at me, shook his head, and walked out. The kids roared with their pleasure. Kids learn to laugh at themselves and their mistakes as well as to laugh *with* one another. A certain sense of acceptance of themselves can come from seemingly silly games. It was amazing to see a high school student, who begrudgingly agrees to a game of gestures, suddenly throwing himself into his actions as he tries to get his teammates to guess what he is acting out amid the smiles and laughter of all involved. A lesson the kids learn is never to be afraid to try something new and be willing to risk when you are in a safe and secure place. Not all groups were full of humor. Some of the topics we talked about included death, funerals, child abuse, teen pregnancy, breaking the law, and many other serious topics.

No chapter on humor would be complete without discussing kids' attempts at being humorous. Unfortunately, many kids have learned to be the "clown" using inappropriate humor to gain the attention of their peers as well as adults in their lives. In my work with kids, I felt it was important that they knew appropriate humor and could recognize the limits that go beyond what is funny. Children learn humor like they learn everything else, by what they see and hear from others. Unless they have appropriate humor modeled to them, they will not know where to begin and either will not attempt humor or do it inappropriately. The difference between a bully or a cruel person and a friend can be in the way they tease and the way they tell jokes. A friend has learned teasing is only humor when it is accepted. The bully, instead, uses teasing as a form of harassment. Likewise, a friend has learned a joke can be funny only if it is in good taste and not offensive or abusive to the people being addressed. Wow, no wonder kids get confused. There is a lot more to humor than just being funny.

In my groups with kids, I often had a time for sharing at the beginning or end of each session. This gave the kids an opportunity to share something personal, tell a joke, or play a trick on the group. I have found out, when kids are allowed to practice and try out humor in the group, they soon learn to be comfortable with it and also know what is appropriate. A joke that isn't funny often gets a remark like "Is that all there is?" With a little guidance, we would help them understand that something was missing in their joke. Then we can look together at what would make it more humorous. Likewise, if a joke were inappropriate, we would gently guide them to a more appropriate type of humor. Then we would let them know what was offensive or out of place. On the other hand, it is hard to describe the joy on kids' faces when they have told a joke that others haven't heard before and hear the laughter and see the smiles. Most kids are awkward in their initial attempts but become more confident and self-assured as they adapt to their style of humor. Whether in a group or individually, I would always try to nurture a kid's sense of humor, for it can be one of their most valuable assets in later life.

When I think kids attempt at humor, April Fools' Day always come to mind. Every year that day brings more of the same, and every year I still seem to fall for their tricks. Sometimes I think God blessed me with my naivety so I could easily fall prey to the humor of kids. They would squeal in delight after they would tell me something serious, watch my reaction, and then smile and say, "April Fools'!"

Other attempts at humor that come to my mind that had happened quite often to me include the following. Kids would tell me I had something on my shirt, only to flip me with their fingers when I looked. They would tell me something that would get my serious attention, then they would smile and say, "Gotcha!"

What I have learned is vulnerability to a child's humor is a way of showing affection while reinforcing their attempts at being funny. It is important to let them know when their humor crosses the line and becomes inappropriate.

As I recall how the humor has touched me each day I have worked with kids, I have a sense of warmth inside that makes me smile. It was that special effect kids had on me that made my job so fruitful and fulfilling. Where else can you spend so much of your time smiling and laughing, enjoying the friendship and love of all those around you? It certainly helps lighten the load of pain, problems, and conflict that was also a part of my work with children. Thank God for humor, for their sake and for mine.

Chapter Seven
Study and Discussion Guide

1. What do you think of the old saying, "Kids say the funniest things"?

2. Because kids are learning as they grow, many of the things they say are serious for them but very funny for the listener. Give some examples of your experiences with kids.

3. Is it important to never laugh at kids when they do funny things unintentionally? Describe the damage that can be done if we laugh at them.

4. It is important that as adults, we can model how to handle our mistakes and be able to laugh at our silly misstatements or projects where we are wrong in some ways. How important is it for us to recognize those mistakes as they happen? It models that it is OK to laugh at yourself, and laughing together can be for all.

5. Talk about kids' attempts at telling jokes and how we can be helpful in letting them know what is appropriate.

6. How do puppet groups for young children and small groups for older kids help in giving them a place to see the mistakes of others and to make some of their own in a place of safety?

EIGHT

Trauma in the School

Trauma in our schools is unpredictable, but it is also inevitable. It is not *if* trauma will hit each of our schools; it, instead, is *when* it will happen. Trauma may come in many different forms, but the common denominator is the impact it has on the children it affects. Be it death of an elderly grandparent of one of the younger children or the loss of a parent for a year or more as they serve in the military, loss affects the entire family, and each member responds to it differently.

As Helen Kübler Ross, in her book *On Death and Dying*, so vividly describes grief as a process for each of us, how we walk through it in our personal journey is as different as each person who experiences it. She talks about the stages of grief and how each stage can be different for every individual. People can be stuck in any one of the stages and never realize they are. They may think they have worked their way through the process when they really have not. Sometimes it takes years and at times successful counseling to realize the stages they did not complete and how it has affected their lives.

This is just a taste of the enormity of trauma in our lives and how it is not a one-time event that is over when it no longer appears to be happening in our life.

When I first became a school social worker, very few of the schools had crisis teams, and those that did focused primarily on trauma in the high schools. Even then it was usually only in the larger schools and only if recent trauma had affected their school. It was one of those situations that you only deal with it after it has happened to your school or community. Even then formal crisis teams were not always formed.

In my first year as a school social worker, I had a baptism by fire in my first week at one of my smaller high schools. I received a call from my school psychologist who was at one of my schools and said there had just been a terrible accident, killing one student and seriously injuring two others, who had been transported to our nearest trauma center in Sioux Falls, South Dakota.

The school psychologist was overwhelmed and felt inadequate in dealing with the situation so he asked me to come immediately.

By the time I got to the school, a decision had been made to send the students home, and I met with the principal and then met with the teachers together as a group. The teachers were all having a difficult time, and I spent several hours with them as a group, helping them deal with their feelings and then giving them guidelines for working with the children in the school. Although the immediate focus was on the high school, I also arranged a meeting with the superintendent and elementary counselor to discuss the effects on the younger children as well.

Listening to the feelings of the children was the most important thing for the teachers to do, and sharing that the sense of loss was also felt by the adults. Not only were kids affected by the current trauma, but it also brought back other traumas, such as death of parents, being in foster care, abusive situations, and many more. These students had to deal with previous events all over again as well as with the current tragedy. When the students came back to school, the teachers were better prepared to deal with their grief and feelings of loss. The teachers were taught not to treat the situation like nothing had happened and immediately go back to regular scheduling and expect everyone to function normally. Certainly, returning to normalcy was important but could only happen after the trauma was effectively dealt with.

Over a period of twenty-five years, my schools came a long way in planning and preparing for the inevitable trauma that was to occur. Now almost all schools have trauma teams that meet on a regular basis and have created extensive plans for methods of dealing with the trauma when it occurs. All district counselors, AEA social workers and school psychologists, building principals, and all at-risk personnel were part of the team as well as local ministers who could be called in when a traumatic event occurred. The advanced planning prepared the schools for handling a traumatic event when it happened.

Trauma could come in many ways. Probably the most common is car accidents, when one or more students are killed and possibly additional students are injured. Often these accidents occur at night, so the other students cannot be notified until the next morning. A crisis team meeting will often be held before school starts so the staff can be aware and ready to deal with the reaction of the students. The building principal will usually assemble his crisis team so everything is in place when the students arrive. Either the school principal or counselor will usually make the announcement to the student body, and all teachers and other personnel will be ready to handle the immediate reaction. A car accident becomes more difficult if drinking has been involved because of the additional emotional impact on the students. Often a lot of guilt is involved if their friends think they could have prevented the drinking or if a designated driver had been available. The whole issue of driving while drinking complicates the initial trauma of the deaths. Multiple deaths and injuries are often more difficult to deal with than single deaths. The crisis team is there to help for the moment, but the aftermath of the trauma can have lasting effects for many of the students and adults as well.

Other traumatic events can include ATV accidents, where the off-road vehicle collides with a car while crossing the road. These accidents often include younger teens and sometimes also involve a passenger. If a passenger is killed, the driver suffers from survivor's guilt and can often be blamed for the accident by some of his peers. Shooting accidents can also involve survivor's guilt if one young hunter has accidently shot and killed one of his peers. These accidents are particularly difficult for students to handle, as they feel they were preventable.

Suicide is another common trauma among teens, and it usually comes as a surprise to students, teachers, and parents as well. At times potential warning signs are overlooked, and the individual may be depressed or upset over circumstances in their lives. There is often a lot of second-guessing and what-if and if-only questions asked by the students. Suicide is one of the most difficult deaths for the students to comprehend and for them to respond to. Often memorials are set up for the student to honor his life, but it is important not to overstate his life to the extent of minimizing the tragedy of a preventable death. Students, parents, and teachers have a difficult time dealing with a death that was not necessary. Other tragedies could include drowning, other accidents, and sudden death from illnesses.

One common denominator is the trauma continues long after the crisis team has left. This adds to the necessity of counselors and social workers to nurture the students and staff alike as they continue to deal with the grief and loss that comes with the trauma. Individual or group counseling is often effective in dealing with the students.

Other trauma includes the death of a teacher and the emotions that brings out in the students, whether elementary or secondary. I recall when a sixth-grade teacher died after being absent for several weeks. Many of the students went to the funeral with their parents and grieved in that way. What was difficult for many students was to go back into their classroom and have the teacher's personal effects still in the classroom. This made many of the students uncomfortable, and it was hard for them to get over her death or to accept it while the classroom remained the same.

Dealing with the assorted traumas in the school is an important part of the school social worker's daily job. Being there for a student who just needs to cry or become angry as a way of dealing with circumstances they do not understand is a very important way of helping kids work their way through the grieving process. Dealing with feelings within groups keep kids from feeling isolated and helps them understand that other kids feel the same way they do. School social workers can be that glue that can help hold kids together during the worst of times and help with the healing process so they can go on with their lives.

Trauma will always happen in our schools, and the school social worker, together with crisis teams, can help deal with it when it happens within their school.

Chapter Eight
Study and Discussion Guide

1. Why do I say it is *when* and not *if* trauma will hit each school district?
2. Describe methods now used to prepare for traumatic events at each school.
3. Briefly talk about what needs to happen after the trauma event to deal with kids who continue to struggle with it.
4. Name the different types of trauma schools have to deal with.
5. Describe prior events that could be triggered by a traumatic event at the school.

The Wonderful Warmth of a Child's Love

By now, you can tell the affection I have for the children I worked with in the fascinating arena of the educational system. This chapter will focus on the many ways the warmth of a child can touch each one of us when we allow it to permeate into our inner being. These kids can touch our every sense and can affect our hearts, minds, and souls. It's a shame that some who work in the school system have become so intent on their subject matter that they don't see the obvious. There is a real caring human being waiting to be taught, cared for, and nurtured in a setting that should be safe for everyone. Don't get me wrong, in no way am I intimating that teachers and school personnel do not care. I'm only saying some of them may have lost the energy and insight and their willingness to take risks because *they have tried too often in vain to be everything for everybody*. But even for these few teachers, there is still hope that they can regain that special touch of love that creates a certain bond between teacher and student. All of us who have worked within the school system can have a positive effect on our kids. Even more importantly, we can be transformed over again, energized by the kids we work with. We just need to spend more of our time and energy loving them, accepting them, and reaping the joy of watching them grow.

In a world where teachers are now expected to be surrogate parents, nurses, dietitians, disciplinarians, social workers, counselors, and who knows what else, it is no wonder frustration can set in. But as I've learned from many wise and wonderful teachers, when you sit back and receive the many gifts given out of love by the kids, it again becomes so much easier to deal with the added pressure, responsibility, heartache, and pain, which are all part of teaching kids today. If we can see the goodness, the talent, the potential, and the love through the various labels and disabilities our kids bring to the table, then it will no longer matter if they have autism, ADHD, learning disability, mental disability, behavioral disability, or any other disability. Our patience, kindness, tolerance, and love can help overcome any disability at any time. Trust me on this one.

In seeing our kids every day, many of the more subtle examples of their love will pass you by without being noticed. If, however, we are in tune with our kids and can recognize the little ways their love is shown, we can experience an almost continuous display of kids' love within our schools. It can be expressed in caring, in playing, in protecting, in sharing, in laughter, in tears, in compassion, in joy. Love from kids is that special communication that often is without words, which shows the relationships they have with the world around them. Quiet observation and unconditional acceptance of these kids as they are can reveal more love than you could ever imagine.

In the many years I worked with children in the school setting, I have learned the atmosphere created for kids in each building can have a tremendous impact on all involved. If the setting is cold and impersonal, focusing only on structure and "learning," quite often the kids will also seem impersonal and devoid of feelings. The staff will also seem immune to the real feelings around them. Kids learn quickly when it is not OK to show sadness or joy, conflict or pride, love or anger. These schools may have good academic standing, but it doesn't take a rocket scientist to recognize something is missing. On the other hand, where the atmosphere is one of acceptance, caring, and love, it is amazing the difference in relationships that evolve and develop not only between students and teachers, but also between teachers and parents. I am grateful to have been blessed with many schools that have this positive loving attitude toward children.

I have found the principal of each building is one major factor in modeling and projecting the atmosphere the building provides for its kids. Everyone knows the principal is the person in charge of discipline and managing the rules of the district. Many see the principal as the pulse of the building, the barometer for acceptance and giving of love between faculty and kids. One principal I worked with called himself the captain of his ship (school), and the image he projected was of a kindly and caring captain who was very concerned for his shipmates (kids). This principal always shared his lunch with students and also made it a point to be in the halls as children passed by. He was visible in the classrooms, lunchrooms, and recesses. Many times I would hear him compliment and encourage kids as well as just chat with them. For sure, when discipline was needed, he could deal with it but always fairly, sternly, and without judgment. The kids in his building felt their principal cared for them, and their willingness to work within the rules showed their respect for the "captain." In this building, there was no stigma attached to going to the principal's office. By highlighting his love, rather than his authority, he established an atmosphere beneficial to the students and faculty.

In many of the other buildings, particularly elementary buildings, principals have, in their way, set a special example for their staff and the kids. They have shown a warmth and acceptance to all in their building. One of my elementary principals several years ago had a reputation as a tough character, and he certainly gave me that impression when I was transferred to his building. He let me know, in no uncertain terms, he was happy with his previous social worker and did not understand or like the change. He also let me know promptness on my part was expected and communication to him of what I did and who I worked with was imperative. I went home that night and asked myself, "What am I getting into?"

As the weeks went by, he must have observed my mannerism with students, staff, and parents and seemed to be lightening up some. I still wasn't sure about him until I saw him one day at recess, wiping the tear from a young girl's face and tenderly talking to her and reassuring her. After that, I paid close attention to his interaction with kids, and I saw a love for children permeated his entire being. Often he would read to a small group or play ball with a few kids at recess. I noticed he was always available in the halls between classes and at lunch and other free times. During this time, he would kid and encourage, tease in a friendly way, laugh, smile, and give out hugs. My opinion of him changed immensely as I continued to know him better. I became very fond of this gruff but grandfatherly image of his. He also changed his feeling about me, and we came to like and respect each other greatly. The bottom line is kids felt loved in his building, and as I found out, so did his staff.

Many of my schools do special things for kids, but one school had a unique way to help every child feel special every day. The staff, including teachers, counselors, AEA personnel, teacher assistants, and administration, would meet every bus every morning and greet all the kids as they entered school. These kids would always receive a smile, a wave, or a hug every morning. No matter how their morning went, once they got off that bus, the welcome was there for everyone. The counselor at the school had an open-door policy and was available for kids whenever he wasn't in a session. He always had a positive relationship with the kids and let them know they were all special. This counselor had a specialty in play therapy and was able to help many kids and their families as they worked through problems in their lives. His specialty made him an excellent counselor, but his special love for kids made him an excellent human being. With him taking the lead, this school made special efforts to show their kids they were loved and cared for. The building principal and the rest of the staff encouraged and reinforced the atmosphere that had been created for kids. Of all the buildings I have worked in, this is the only school where students and teachers were high-fiving each other as they walked through the halls. When we realize the family situations many children come from, it's heartwarming to know understanding and care were given to kids every day at school. It's no wonder so many of these kids feel comfortable in sharing their love and care with one another and the staff. If we want kids to feel free to express those special talents and gifts, we must model that expression of love and care for them.

Many of the other schools I have worked in also have ways to make their kids feel wanted and cared for. The addition of breakfast has been one of the ways of impacting kids. Not only do we know they have had a good meal to start their day, but they also have positive social interaction with other kids and the adults supervising. It also gives them a sense acceptance and well-being. Counselors and teachers play key roles in their interaction with kids. When the attitude toward the kids is one that builds up their self-esteem and recognizes each child's worth, then you know more than academics are taught at that school.

For many years, I have watched the "Teacher of the Year Awards" on the Disney Channel and have marveled at the energy, enthusiasm, and creativity of these teachers. There is no doubt in my mind the kids in their classrooms feel loved and comfortable enough to take those risks of trying something new with their teachers. Many of the teachers in my schools show that same energy and love for their work and their kids. It shows in the loving relationships their kids have with them.

In my first year as a school social worker, I wondered how much of a difference I could make in the lives of my kids. I might only work with them for fifteen to twenty minutes a session individually, twenty to thirty for small groups, and only around forty minutes for classroom groups. Having been a therapist who was used to fifty-minute session in my office or two hours when I went to a client's home, I was rather doubtful of the impact I could have on the many children I worked with. What I found out is kids need consistency and care with follow-through over the years. Even though the amount of time may be limited, the relationship, once established, does not go away but continues to be nurtured through the school year and often in years to come. Many times the impact has been far greater than I had expected; my ability to be kind and genuine with my kids has been a small part in some fantastic changes in their lives. I'd now like to share some of the examples of the love I've received from my kids.

One of the benefits and sometimes drawbacks of being a school social worker was I had the opportunity to work with kids from preschool to high school in several of my districts. I certainly was spread thin in terms of time with the kids, but I could follow them from grade to grade and building to building, so they had a consistency in knowing I still could have contact with them when they went from elementary to middle school and onto high school. One student I worked with was an example of the importance of a consistent relationship. He has shown his care in many different ways. I started working with him when he was in third grade. Through a series of family visits and a professional evaluation, as well as a month-long hospitalization, he was diagnosed as having childhood autism. Because I traveled this journey with him and his family, I became an important person in his life. He was a very nervous child, as many children with autism are, and I was always careful not to disrupt his classroom when I came to see him. He would often blurt out and announce my presence when I came. I may have been there for the whole group and not just him. After many talks, I felt confident he could handle my entering the classroom without making a fuss. As I entered the room the next time, I could see he noticed me, and there was no visible reaction. He did raise his hand appropriately, and I thought everything was OK. But when the teacher called on him, he excitedly announced, "Mr. Hoye is in the room!"

So much for that lesson. This young man later left to go to middle school and high school that was more focused on life skills. When he heard I had won the state school social worker award, he sent me an e-mail, saying, "You deserve the award and I love you."

When I saw him many years later, he caught me up on how he was doing and then gave me a hug, which was very rare for some children with autism.

I am always surprised at the many ways kids express their love and how innocent and yet so open they are with their expression of feelings. When kids know they are in a safe place, their willingness to share is greatly increased, and you never know what to expect. One year I was working with a fifth-grade student who had been through much pain and turmoil in his life, but he had responded quite well when certain accommodations were introduced into his academic setting. He had never been able to express himself easily, but I have always known he appreciated my help. One day he looked at me and said, "Dave, you've been my friend and counselor for quite a while now, and you've helped me a lot. I think it's about time I learn more about you, so why don't you tell me about yourself?"

I'm sure there was a big smile on my face as I responded to him. I knew he had worked through many of his problems and now wanted to express his care for me.

Elementary kids are so full of love and are continually looking for a caring receiver to give it to. When teachers are responsive to this love, relationships grow. Kids are then touched by learning from the teachers who are willing to receive as well as to give. Have you ever noticed the look on a child's face when they give their teacher a completed piece of work? Regardless of whether it is a written report, a drawing, or a homework assignment, they wait anxiously for the teacher's response. The teacher who responds with kindness and patience has those kids forever as learners in their classroom. A teacher who acts indifferent or rebukes the child has rejected this child's love and maybe the child's best effort and will probably have a resistive child for the remainder of the year. When kids would reach out to me for a hug or a smile or the recognition of a waving hand or a high five, I had better have noticed and responded, or a moment of love has been lost forever. When a child gives a gift, whether it is a piece of gum, a string bracelet, a picture of a horse, or a pencil, it needs to be recognized and responded to positively. This is an act of giving and an act of love. The only thing the child wants in return is a smile or a thank-you from us.

One of my greatest experiences with kids' love was as a coach for the Special Olympics. The Special Olympics is the epitome of competition as it is meant to be. The true spirit of competing means more than winning or losing, and these games make it possible for many children with special needs to have the opportunity for participation in sports. I had the wonderful opportunity to be a coach at several different schools, at the local and state level. The sense of achievement and the pride in their accomplishment was almost universal among the athletes who compete. The love shown among athletes was a model for good sportsmanship. I always saw tremendous growth is these kids who competed in the Special Olympics, in the social aspect as well as the willingness to work and train for their event. Many of these children had not been involved in a regular exercise program and were not involved in other activities. Being Special Olympians gave them the incentive for healthier living and eating as well. Most of all, Special Olympics gave the kids a place where coaches and leaders emphasized respect and kindness for one another. It was also where the kids mixed the excitement of competing with the appropriate ways to win or lose.

On trips to the state competition, I would be the male chaperone for two or three of the male athletes. We had many humorous experiences during these times. I became much more aware of the needs and strengths of these special kids. I continued to share that sense of warmth and love they have for the adults in the world they trust. One boy's parents previously had difficulty getting him to exercise. He had even fought much of the pre-event training. After he won his biking event in Ames, he was so excited and uplifted that the following year he became much more physically active in his daily life. He eagerly trained for the next Special Olympics. His personal growth and social appropriateness also grew tremendously during this time. I attribute at least some of that growth to his success in his competition. To see the hugs and the high-fives and the cheers for one another and other teams is truly heartwarming. To see the tears of joy and the smiles as they stand on the awards stand makes our efforts worthwhile. It was rewarding to return to Ames every year and to see kids from all the schools I had been a coach for previously. The kids from other teams would remember me and relate to me as if I hadn't left. It also imprints in my mind the difference we adults make in a child's life. These relationships, once established, never go away.

Many of the groups I co-facilitated would work on social skills and basic friendship skills. Over time, I noticed the interaction that happens in small groups can lead to long-term friendships. The willingness to risk, to share feeling, to disclose painful experiences, and to join in laughter and fun seemed to radiate a trust and love within the group that would remain long after the group was discontinued. Likewise, as a group leader, once a child has been in a group with me, the trust was established for a later time when needing help or comfort.

In one of those classroom groups, at the end of the year, we would have the students write positive comments about each of their classmates; the teachers and leaders in the group would do the same. The teachers would then make a book for each of us with all their comments. The kids received a sense of worth and accomplishment from their classmates that did more for their self-esteem than any other group exercise in which I was involved. The adults were impacted as well and often would have tears in their eyes when they read their books. We certainly knew our efforts throughout the year were given back to us many times over. When love is given, it can also be received.

Another classroom had some unique characteristics. This special education classroom had kids from first grade through fourth grade and varied from mild disabilities to quite involved physical or mental disabilities. Ordinarily, I would subdivide such a class into smaller groups that were more alike in age and ability levels. However, because of the special interaction of the kids in this classroom, I kept them all together. If there was ever an argument for the old single classroom school, I certainly saw it in this classroom. The older children took care of the younger kids, academically and socially, while the higher-ability kids showed tremendous patience with the lower-ability kids. At Christmas one year, the teacher focused on the gift of time, and these kids poured their hearts out in sharing about their time with families and friends. At the same time, they showed by example as they shared time with their classmates. I always left this building with a warm feeling of love in my heart; whether I had followed my plan for the day, the goal of caring and sharing was always accomplished.

As I have shared before, working with puppets brings a whole new dimension of a young child's love. They are all enthralled by my fuzzy little friends. They look forward to the time they could give those hugs and love and then share them with one another. In using puppets, I found a safe and sure way for kids to express their feelings of love without risk of rejection or impropriety. With the puppets, I also was able to show appropriateness of hugs of when and with whom they could be shared. I also would show them other appropriate ways to show friends affection, such as hugs, hand waves, and high-fives. This gave them alternative ways to greet and show care to people around them.

No chapter about kids' love would be complete without exploring the messages kids are trying to send us. We can't live and thrive in a world devoid of love and care. These messages need to be seen and accepted by the adults who spend the most time with these kids. They also need to be modeled by parents, teachers, and other adults in their lives. Kids need to feel loved and be cared for during the time they are in our care. The giving and receiving of love with our kids can be one of the most gratifying parts of our careers. It can also be a catalyst for change with many of the children we work with. As important as academics are to schools, if the kids do not feel nurturing, joy, and fun in their relationships, then the value of their learning has been diminished. Those of us who are educators have the responsibility to nurture what some children already have and to give others what they need to feel worthwhile. No matter what the circumstances may be, love is never wasted on kids, nor is it ever given in vain. What we receive from them in return is that wonderful warmth of a child's love.

Chapter Nine
Study and Discussion Guide

1. Agree or disagree with this statement: Love can almost always be found at school in relationships between children and adults. Discuss why you feel as you do.

2. Teachers who are always positive with the children experience the gift of love given to them by their kids. Talk about how you have seen kids openly show they care in your classroom or other setting within the school.

3. Never turn down a small gift given to you by a child and always express your thanks. These gifts are given because of the love and care you have shown them. Give examples you have seen or experienced.

4. Why are puppet groups and small groups fertile ground for the sharing and caring between children and the group leaders?

5. Agree or disagree: Positive behavior support or other similar programs help educational professionals identify positive behavior and acknowledge it.

6. Talk about the love that can be see when working with developmentally disabled students and adults as well.

TEN

Parenting: Kids Can Tell Us All We Need to Know

Throughout my career as a school social worker and family therapist, the dilemma of parenting has been a constant. Many programs espousing various philosophies have been seen as *the answer* for parents looking for the method that will solve their conflicts while turning out "perfect children." Over the years, I have used many effective methods, such as "positive parenting," "active parenting," "parent effectiveness training," "1-2-3-Magic," and components of many other programs. I have found the best parents are those who know their kids well and are willing to listen to them as they show them what it is they need.

Each of our kids is unique and special; the requirements for meeting their needs from cradle to adulthood vary greatly. From a very early age, they tell us what works and what doesn't for them. They will tell you the best methods of discipline, nurturing, and caring for them, if only we will listen and really hear and observe what they are telling us.

Many of the problematic parenting issues that constantly present a struggle can be resolved quite readily when we are able to differentiate between what kids say and what they really mean. When parents concentrate on being "parents," that is adults who are responsible for the well-being and growth of our children throughout their lives, we should not try to be our kid's best friend. When we are parents, it becomes much clearer as to the limits and structure that kids not only want but also need. Too many parents are more concerned with pleasing their children than in addressing their needs in positive yet firm ways. Parents often confuse the need for flexibility, patience, and tolerance for giving in, enabling, or low expectations. Parenting is certainly not easy, and the times we live in make it even more difficult. If we recognize cues our kids give us and listen to what they are telling us verbally and nonverbally, then parenting becomes a much more manageable task.

In every area of a child's life, they tell us what they need. Whether we understand and respond appropriately is another issue altogether. For instance, a nervous new father may feel he is meeting his baby's needs by responding to her crying with another bottle. He knows he has guessed wrong when she throws the bottle across the room and intensifies her crying. If Dad had only searched a little deeper to find to find the wetness in the diaper, he would have known the problem. Likewise, a young child who is yelling he hates us may not need more nurturing but rather may need his parents to follow through on their discipline and not give in to tantrums. A teenager may continue to bug his parents about his curfew, but they need to continue to follow through and not give in. A fourteen-year-old girl may try to get her parents to let her date, even though she really wants them to stick to their rules and make her wait. As much as she wants to be like the other girls whose parents allow and even encourage early dating, she knows in her heart she's not ready. She feels secure when her parents set the limits, and she can blame it on them. In so many instances, our kids are telling us they want us to step in and be the "bad guys" so they don't have to tell their friends no and explain why. Parents can be a shield to help kids have enough strength to listen to their heads rather than their hearts. I am sure the many times my daughters refused to go along with friends wishes by saying, "My folks would kill me if I did that."

What they are really saying is "I don't want to do something that I feel is wrong, and I'm glad my parents are willing to be my excuse."

Kids want to be parented; we just need to learn the strange code they use to tell us what they really need.

Teachers and parents and other adults need to remember the importance of modeling to the kids we work with. Kids will imitate what we do much more than what we say. Our message as parents and teachers must be consistent with our actions and deeds. If not, it will be rendered useless and seen as hypocritical and deceitful. Kids look to the adults in their lives for guidance and advice but are more interested how adults handle difficulties in their lives. They watch and see how the adults choose to deal with difficulties in their lives and how they deal with similar situations to what the kids face. Doing only what we say just doesn't cut it with our kids. They want to be parented by example and not just with empty words. Kids tell us all we need to know about what will work for them as far as our parenting. Then they give us that information by how they react to the style and type of parenting we use. Whether we are dealing with discipline, religious beliefs, family lifestyle, recreation, extended family, finances, or any other issue, our kids will look to us for an example, and then they will tell us what works for them and how we need to deal with them. As adults, we often need to admit our mistakes. We need to be honest with our children. It helps kids understand we are not perfect, and we realize they don't have to be either.

One of the most controversial issues of parenting has always been and still is discipline. The opposite ends of the continuum range from strong physical discipline to allowing children to make all their decisions on their actions and attitudes. Kids will be the first to tell us neither of the extremes is effective and that both can have detrimental effects that can last a lifetime. Kids need limits, and they need consequences, but they need be given with sternness and not out of anger. Discipline can and should be an act of love and not an act of violence or fear, nor should it be one of indifference or noncommitment. As much as parents agonize over disciplining their kids and feel inadequate and uncertain in their attempts, the answers are right there in front of them. We need to look at what works for the other people in their lives, such as babysitters, teachers, ministers, and parents of their friends. Discipline should not be seen as a reflection of our worth as parents but rather as a reflection of our love for our children. Through the years, I have worked with a wide variety of "difficult" kids. What I've found that works for all of them is consistency, structure, and unconditional love. Likewise, what doesn't work is physical discipline, fits of anger, power struggles, and ultimatums. If you don't believe me, ask any kid who has difficulties in relationships, and they will affirm what works and what doesn't work.

Kids want consistency, and they want limits set that they know will not be changed at the whim of one of their parents or in a fit of anger or because they feel sorry for them. Discipline needs to meet their challenges to you, but it also needs to be handled calmly and patiently. It needs to have steadfastness and firmness that creates an atmosphere of love. Parents need to take a stand on issues important to them. Kids don't handle a wishy-washy parent very well. They will press this parent to the limit to make him/her take a stand, forcing this parent to back up his/ her threats or promises. Your word needs to be trusted, and any change in your discipline needs to be done through a process of compromising and listening to others' point of view. It should never be because it is easier to give up or give in than it is to follow through. Kids have been "eating" indecisive parents alive for years. It is not because they want to disobey but rather because they want to know what your limits really are and not have interchangeable limits based on their mood or yours. If there is one word I have used with parents over the years, it is *consistency*. Without some essence of consistency, we set our kids up for confusion and resentment. We also set up ourselves up for failure as parents.

Discipline needs to be set by defining limits and consequences and then consistently apply and follow through on what has been set. In a world full of empty promises and uncertainty, our children are asking us to set guidelines and stick to them. Starting from the time our kids are very young, they need to have discipline that is firm yet calm, consistent and yet open to compromise. They need to know it is directed at the child's behavior and not at his/her person. Whether using *1-2-3-Magic* for younger children or *STEP* for adolescents, your discipline needs to be without anger and without putdowns or condemnation. Kids respond to calmness and to quiet but firm follow through on limits. If a child feels guilty, a screaming match only reaffirms their guilt, making them angry and rebellious. If a child has committed a crime, violated school rules, or has disobeyed family rules, parents need to act in accordance with the action of the child supporting any authorities involved. A parent, for example, who "chews out" their child for drinking but then goes to the school board to fight their child's suspension is clearly giving mixed messages. We must love our children despite their mistakes, but we also need for them to suffer the consequences for their actions. Many times, in working with kids who are on probation or have been sent to drug-alcohol treatment, they tell me how many times their parents lied for them or covered up for them when they started getting into trouble. What these parents needed to do was to force them to deal with the consequences. Unfortunately, our prisons are filled with young adults whose parents refused to discipline consistently and instead made excuses and bailed them out time after some time while they were juveniles. Unfortunately, the message was that consequences didn't happen to them.

If I could have only one message to parents about discipline, it is that it is never easy, but it is always necessary to make your kids responsible for their actions while still feeling loved and supported by you. Kids do not want to make all their decisions, and they do not want to be unsupervised or left on their own. When their peers are trying to influence them, kids want us to know where they are, who they are with, and what they are doing. Unfortunately, when parents refuse to set those limits, kids will run wild outside of any supervision or control. Only then will they get their parents' attention through their negative actions. A major point for all of us to understand is our children will grow up with or without our discipline. However, the difference in parents' decision-making will affect the rest of their child's life. How we choose to discipline is probably our most important responsibility as parents. Our kids are waiting for us to make a choice of being active, positive disciplinarians or uninvolved, passive, or reactive disciplinarians. While it is our choice, our children will have to live with the consequences of our decision.

When we ask our kids what they need most from their parents, the most common answer is time. Whether our kids are preschoolers or high schoolers, the best way to nurture them is by giving them time with each of their parents. How we spend that time with them will determine the relationship we will have with our kids. We need to view each child as a special gift from God, given to us to shape and mold from a precious baby to becoming a productive and positive adult. The most important ingredient in a child's growth is the relationship with his parents. Our kids learn their coping skills, interests, strengths, and weaknesses from us. They receive their sense of self-worth and value by how we nurture and care for them. They learn how to handle conflict, how to spend free time, how to deal with crises, and how to give and receive love. Who we are as parents is reflected on our children in every aspect of their lives; the amount of and quality of time spent with them help determine their view of family and relationships. The child who receives things rather than time quickly realizes material possessions are more important in their family than relationships. Their sense of value will be directed toward material gains rather than in successful relationships. A child whose parents have always been involved in their activities and in their daily lives will know the value of relationships and caring for one another. They also will know who their parents really are and will have learned the values their parents live by rather than only guessing what those values are.

Even though adolescents may balk at time spent, they still expect you at each game, school play, band concert, or speech contest and will be disappointed if you are not there. When a kid can look back at their childhood, the memories of mom or dad teaching them to ride their first bike, playing catch together, or baiting their hook on their first fishing trip will be remembered. They will also remember their parents teaching them to drive and taking pictures of them at their prom. These things take time on the part of their parents, but they pay tremendous dividends in terms of memories and values your kids will have forever. When parents don't spend time with their children, somebody else will, and the child's values will reflect those of the people who shared time with them. If that's a scary thought, then perhaps, as parents, we all need to readjust our priorities and remember that we chose to be parents and our kids did not have any choice of coming into this world. Giving time to our kids can be the most joyous part of our parenting. But time can slip by quickly if we are not prioritizing it for our kids.

It's kind of sobering when we look at the most important aspect of our parenting. Our children are going to be mirror images of who we are as human beings. If we are honest and open in our dealings with others, then our children will learn to be assertive and to let people know how they feel. If we have a strong spiritual commitment and show it in our church involvement and our treatment of others, our children will learn the importance of God in their lives. If we have a strong work ethic, our children learn the importance of responsibility and hard work. If we laugh a lot and appreciate humor, our children will appreciate laughter and know how to have fun. If we place a value on our family, our children will not have a problem being involved in family activities. Our kids learn from who we are, and they reflect those values we practice in our lives. So if there is one key to good parenting, I guess it is to be the kind of person you'd like your child to be. It won't take a miracle to make it happen, only time, care, and love.

Below are some of the primary parenting issues and a short summary of what kids want from us and what we, parents, need to do.

Showing Love and Affection

Kids want and need physical and verbal affirmation of our love, and they need those affirmations consistently and often. Parents need to always remember to tell their kids they are loved by them and be willing to hug them and give positive touch in happy and sad times. We need to take the time to reaffirm our love for them and not be afraid to show that love within the family and the community. Even though kids reach an age where they might act embarrassed or shy away from these affirmations, they still really want and need them.

Discipline

Kids want consistent and immediate consequences for their actions. They want to know they are still loved despite what they have done but that their negative actions will not be accepted or condoned. Kids want limits, and they want them to be enforced. They also want examples modeled by their parents. Parents need not give in prematurely, nor should they overreact to their child's actions. They need to be consistent and firm in dealing with them. Parents need to support their kids but also need to back any involved authorities in dealing with consequences.

Drinking and Drugs

Kids want us to say no and want us to intervene in the peer pressure they receive. Kids want to be able to use their parents as an excuse for not going along with their peers. Kids want parents to enforce "no" and give immediate and strong consequences when they have slipped and been involved with drugs or alcohol. Kids want parents to support them but not fight authorities and intervene in punishment or consequences from school or juvenile authorities. Parents also need to practice what they preach and not abuse alcohol or use illegal drugs. Parents need to support their kids but also support school and community officials when their child has been caught violating rules. If we support the consequences given by the school or community, we tell our kids we will not tolerate their behavior.

Dating

Kids want limits set on their involvement with relationships, for they are uncertain of their abilities to handle them. They want limits on time and frequency of involvement and parameters around time spent alone with these boy or girl friends. Parents need to be understanding of their kids' desire for relationships, but they must not push them toward dating at too early an age. Parents need to encourage using their home as a place for their children's friends to be and encourage several friends or couples being together rather than just one to one. When parents are not negative toward their kids' choices, relationships will become stronger. When parents are negative, a rebellious attitude is created.

Sex

Kids want to know about the realities of sex and its dangers. They want their folks to tell them the truth rather than hearing distorted versions from their friends. Kids want and need to know about AIDS, about contraception, and about abstinence. They want to know your values as parents. Kids want you to know if they have had sex and need your support, not your approval. They need to know they are OK even though they have made a mistake. They also need to know you love them even if you don't approve of their sexual choices. Parents need to be comfortable and willing to discuss all issues of sex with their kids; they need to help them sort through their options. Parents need not overreact with hurt and anger when your kids have chosen to become sexually active and have told you. Parents need to show their love, even when you disapprove their choices. Parents need to let their kids know their values and why they feel as they do. Parents need not have a different standard for their daughters from their sons.

Driving and Cars

Kids want to know as much about driving from their parents before they start to learn. Kids want their parents to be involved in teaching them to drive and want to learn from their experiences. Kids want limits set on their driving and want limits set on car ownership. Kids do not want everything given to them just because they ask. Kids want you to trust their driving and their judgment. They also want to know your experiences and how you handled different driving situations. Kids want to know the risks and how to handle them from drunk-driving to driving on ice or snow, in rain or fog, or at night. Parents need patience and trust but also willingness to set limits and to say no in certain circumstances. Parents need to show confidence in their kids but not so much as to endanger them by allowing them into situations they are not ready to handle. Parents should not just give their kids a new car or even a used car but rather should have them earn it or buy it with them. Parents need to show kids limits in terms of expectations as well as actions.

Friends

Kids want you to know their friends and want them to be welcome in their home. They want friendship modeled to them by you so they know the appropriate way of treating their friends. They also want to know why when you don't approve. Your kids need to know they can invite friends, even if their parents don't particularly like them. Those friends who are not good influences often will refuse to spend time in your kids' home. You need to set limits for your kids' involvement outside of your home with friends and always be willing to check out where they are going and with whom. Your kids may get very angry at you for checking but will eventually respect you for caring. As parents, you need to open your home to your kids' friends and be involved in the many activities that involve your children and their friends. The more visible you are, the more comfortable your kids' friends will become. As parents, resist being judgmental of your kids' friends but continue to set limits for your kids, regardless of the freedom their friends may have.

Work and Recreation

Your kids want to know the importance of work and chores. They want you to not only give them responsibilities, but also to teach them with patience as they learn to do these chores. Your kids want to see how you play and enjoy your leisure. They want to have those activities modeled for them and with them so they will learn to enjoy them as well. Parents need to expose their children to work and play at an early age, demonstrating the value in both. A parent who works with his children and enjoys recreation with them models a balanced lifestyle that is healthy for the whole family.

Religion and Moral Values

Your kids want you to be an example to them and to model the values that are important. If church and religion are important to you, your kids want to be taught and shown why. They don't want you to pawn them off on others for that instruction but for you to have an active part in it. As parents, our best method of instilling values in our children is by living those values ourselves. Our beliefs and our moral ethics are passed on to our children by how we live our daily lives.

***

Parenting is a wonderful gift given to us at the birth of our children. To be effective at it, we need to only look toward our kids and listen to what they need from us. From a tiny infant to a grown man or woman, they continue to tell us what they need from us as parents.

Chapter Ten
Study and Discussion Guide

1. Name some of the parent training programs often used by the schools to help train parents.
2. In what ways do kids tell us what they need from us as parents?
3. How can we tell if we are using effective parenting methods with our kids?
4. Even effective parenting is just a guide for our kids. Kids can still misbehave and get into trouble. Why?
5. What are some of the topics and areas we need to be aware of?
6. How do we let our children know we are listening to what they think they need?

ELEVEN

Hope: A Lesson for All of Us

In my thirty years of working with kids, I've found a deep sense of hope shining through in a world full of danger and pain and abuse and stress. Despite the many hardships children undergo in today's world, those of us who spend our days intertwined in the lives of children can't help but feel hope rather than this despair as we see the strength of character and resilience of kids regardless of the conditions in which they live and the educational handicaps they must endure. Kids, indeed, are the future of our world. Despite the challenges they face, I feel our world can, indeed, feel the same hopefulness for the future as our parents felt was when we were children. True, some of the innocence may be gone, and children face reality at an earlier age, but with the willingness to share and care for one another, along with the power of a child's will to survive and endure, they emerge successful. We observe this each day as we watch children battle huge odds. They can still win in the classroom and on the playing field and at home. Kids have hope where we would see none. They use that hope as a catalyst to survive and thrive in a different world. We—educators, parents, and adults in their lives—have the responsibility to reinforce that hope and encourage it until it becomes their reality. In this chapter, I will look at true experiences of families and children where hope made a difference in their lives. Also, we will look at the importance of key people in the lives of kids; how their hope is transformed into the necessary strength a child needs to be successful.

We have all seen children who are so discouraged that they seem to have given up. We may not always recognize the problem as a loss of hope. It may be presented by acting out, resistance to authority, not responding to help, or by defiance. We may not know the child's history of failure or how many times they have repeatedly tried, only in their minds to be put down or set aside. We have no idea of the emotional pressures a particular child has from their home situation or how many losses they have suffered in their lives. What we do know is we have a child who, for whatever the reason, is no longer functioning within our school setting and doesn't seem to care.

These kids we see every day are not only at risk for dropping out of school, but also for dropping out of life. When a child has given up hope, he will no longer function within our school setting without some quick and effective action. He will resort to anything that will numb their pain or hurt or give them some false hope to grab onto. These kids are at risk for drug or alcohol abuse, gang membership, early pregnancy, suicide, involvement in crime, cult membership, and anything else that would give them a sense of belonging or the potential for easing their pain. Regardless of their age, these kids are not going to be saved unless someone positive in their lives can instill hope and guide them through enough successes that hope becomes a reality and a goal for their lives. It doesn't take a major miracle, nor does it just happen, but the effects of renewed hope can result in a miraculous change in the child's life.

These kids are right in front of us each day in school. Before they fade away, drop out, or alienate everyone within reach, we must recognize them and find an adult who can reestablish trust and become their advocate in school and in life. Unfortunately, we are all aware of the kids who have dropped out of school and have become dependent on drugs or alcohol. Those kids who continue to violate the law may wind up in prison or possibly commit suicide. The media makes sure we are all aware of these kids. However, there are many more stories of successful intervention we probably would never hear about unless we have been involved in those interventions. Many kids are brought back to hope because of caring adults in their lives. Whether at school or within the community, these adults make the difference between giving up and continuing the battle, ultimately between success and failure.

Most children have a natural optimism and a sense of hopefulness that is strong and resilient and can withstand a great deal of adversity. We have all seen little children consoling their parents after a family tragedy or misfortune, reassuring them that things will get better. Regardless of their situations, kids usually begin with the feeling that their hopes and dreams can become a reality. I have been amazed at their ability to maintain hope even in the most devastating of situations. Kids do not begin by being despondent or without hope or sullen or angry. Instead, they are more like a flower about to bloom. They only need nourishment and nurturing to bring them to their potential. We, the adults in their lives, are charged with the responsibility of being the nurturers who can encourage and reinforce that hope so it can be brought to fruition. We never know when a friendly smile or a pat on the back or a word of encouragement or some help with a difficult task may be the difference between continuing hope or losing it. Standing up for a child who feels defenseless and building a sense of esteem, which has become very fragile, for a child are the things we can do each day within our schools. We need not to miss those opportunities because we cannot see them. It is easy to assume only the kids who struggle outwardly need nurturing, but at times some of our most successful kids have become perfectionist and extremely critical of themselves. They are as much in need of support as the kids with more obvious needs. Hope does not continue without nurturing, but fortunately, it does not die easily. As adults in kids' lives, we need to remember their hopefulness need not conform to our ideals or goals for them. We need not to "rain on their parade" by putting them down or minimizing something they are truly excited about. Many of our kids receive their hopefulness from things outside of school. Unless the source of their hope is encouraged, we will never see it transferred to include school achievement. Hope comes from a feeling of worth and a sense of being OK that sustains them on days that don't go well for them. Every time we acknowledge that sense of worth and reinforce it, we strengthen their hope and willingness to struggle through tough times.

While at a workshop several years ago, the featured speaker shared a remarkable story about hope and the difference a person can have in a child's life. A young girl who seemed to be bright and cheerful suddenly went through a series of losses in her life. First, her mother died and then her father. This affected her personality, her self-esteem, and her coping ability. She became a child who didn't care about school and started being withdrawn and resistive in the classroom. In fourth grade, her teacher had to fight feelings of dislike for this girl who suddenly was no longer a pleaser and at times would be surly and disruptive. Even though the teacher was aware of her losses, it was still hard to be supportive and caring when those efforts seemed to be rejected. She resolved, however, to continue to try to instill hope and confidence in this little girl who was mired in hopelessness. The girl's peer relationships had also deteriorated, and she was often teased or put down. That Christmas, the teacher had the children draw names, and she made sure the little girl had her name. The girl brought her teacher an obviously worn pin that had belonged to her mother and a partially used bottle of perfume. This gift was obviously an attempt to reach out and reestablish a relationship with an adult. The other children, however, started to make fun of her and chided her for her choice of gift. For some unknown reason, the teacher suddenly felt a tremendous sense of empathy and love for this little girl. She also felt anger at the reaction of the other children. She proudly put on the pin and dabbed a little perfume and praised the little girl for her thoughtfulness and willingness to share what had been her mother's. She also firmly but gently taught the other children a lesson about giving and about acceptance of one another. From that time on, the child seemed to show improvement, and the teacher spent extra time and effort to catch her up on her studies and to restore that old desire to learn and achieve. By the end of the school year, the girl had regained much of her old spark in school and was again becoming an excellent student. What happened after that was remarkable and undeniably shows the impact we in education can have on a child.

This girl wrote her former teacher a series of letters, thanking her for her care and her willingness to give hope when she had none. The letters came after her graduation from high school, college, and then medical school, all with honors. The final letter was the announcement of her engagement to be married and a request that this teacher come to the wedding and sit in the spot reserved for the bride's mother. An act of kindness and a desire to protect and preserve the child's dignity turned into a catalyst that reversed the trend of hopelessness and restored hope into this child's life. What seemed to be so little meant so much to this child that it made an impact that lasted forever. Certainly, many other people touched this child's life after this teacher, but without that first intervention, who knows what direction that child would have gone?

Throughout my many years in education, I have seen countless incidents of the special teacher changing the direction of a child's life with their kindness and support and innate ability to bring out the best in a child, reinforcing each of the child's strengths. One such special teacher was a fifth-grade teacher. Over the years, many children with learning disabilities struggled through their classes with many difficulties and the need for modifications for them to be successful. Then in the fifth grade, it suddenly seemed as if their learning problems disappeared, and they all experienced a success contrary to their previous educational history. What really happened is they encountered a teacher who used multimodal teaching methods and found a way to teach to the strengths of each individual child. By using these varied methods, she was challenging the good students while reaching out to those who had previously struggled, teaching to their individual learning styles. She certainly did not eliminate the student's learning disabilities, but she offered hope and gave them a taste of success that, in many cases, sustained through their upcoming struggles. She treated each child as an individual and valued them for their gifts and talents she uncovered and reinforced. One of the many students for whom she made a special difference was my daughter. She has a learning disability and experienced one disastrous year after another in elementary school until she came to this teacher's class. This teacher would encourage children to recognize their worth as a student and a person, giving them hope that school could get better and be a safe and enjoyable place for each child to learn.

One of the most common yet misunderstood reason for hopelessness in children comes from being stuck somewhere in the grief process. Whether it is caused by experiences of death in the family, divorce, or by other traumatic losses, it can be debilitating and devastating for a child. Unless the child receives understanding and nurturing, it could have lasting effects. Unfortunately, schools are as guilty as parents, court systems, and communities in assuming the grief process passes naturally and that kids do not need any special treatment. For this reason, we often see students who lose interest in school, peer relationships, and their favorite activities. We often blame the child rather than looking for a solution. One of my good friends was an elementary guidance counselor who always did a wonderful job in recognizing grief in her students and always found ways to deal openly and honestly with it. She enabled her students to recognize their feelings as being normal and to help them work through the areas in which they have become stuck. This counselor has dealt with more than her share of grief, having lost her husband and her eldest son. She is a wonderful example of dealing with her grief and carrying on with her life. She is a person who was full of hope, and her energy and love of life served as a model for her students. This counselor developed small groups for kids dealing with loss and was a major catalyst in the lives of many kids in bridging that gap between hopelessness and hope. Her honesty and willingness to share herself has helped many students realize they are not alone in their grief, and with the help and support of others, they can accept their grief and see a light at the end of the tunnel. She also works with families and helps them understand the importance of recognizing the grief process within themselves and with their children. She assisted them in finding resources that helped them let go of their barriers, turning despair into hope. Part of the secret to sustaining hope is passing it on to others and nurturing those in need with support and love. We all know some special people who are full of hope and willingly model that for all of us. These wonderful people never give up hope, never give in to despair, and never, ever, lose their beliefs in others. What makes them special? If I knew the exact ingredient, I would bottle it and give it to all those without hope, those who see life as a battle and not a challenge. What they all have in common is a true appreciation of life and a childlike faith in the world around them. They give rather than take, focusing on others rather than themselves. They are satisfied with who they are yet are always striving to attain a dream or a vision. They don't look back unless it is to smile at a warm memory. They don't fret about the future, but they enjoy each day as it is given to them. Look at the people in your lives who help nurture a sense of hopefulness, and you will recognize many of the qualities I listed. In addition, most of these people who have hope have a true faith in God or a higher power.

Chapter Eleven
Study and Discussion Guide

1. Many young children always seem filled with hope for the future. Give several explanations for why they may feel this way.
2. Hopeful kids usually enjoy more success in school, academically and socially. Please explain in your words why this may be.
3. What are some of the things that can take hope away from kids?
4. Tell some of the ways we, educators, can tell when a child is losing hope.
5. What may happen to kids who are losing hope?
6. Poor grades and lack of social relationships can lead to hopelessness. What can be done to restore hope to these kids?
7. How likely is hopelessness going to carry over to adulthood?

TWELVE

Even Kids Grow Up

All the kids we work with will eventually grow up. It is our hope someone, somewhere in their lives will have the positive impact necessary to help them grow into productive adults. Parents, teachers, clergy, counselors, and peers all have impact on kids, but eventually, kids make their decisions as they develop into adulthood. As we look at kids in elementary and even in middle school, we can only speculate on their development and the direction their lives will take. We watch with wonder and with admiration how, despite many adversities, kids often grow well beyond our expectations. We never know which kids we have reached with our love, our interventions, or our discipline and in what way they will eventually react and grow. We hope and pray those whose influence was positive will have more impact than those who were negative.

I've had the privilege over the years to see many of the kids I've worked with after they finish school and are on their own. Although many have made bad choices in their lives, it is heartwarming to see those who are having successes in their adult lives. Often adults who have positive impact on kids never see the results of their efforts or realize they made a difference in a kid's life. When you follow kids all the way through school and see their progress, it's easy to see the impact certain teachers or other adults can have in a kid's life.

Some kids seem to grow up despite themselves, and although they seem to disregard any help or advice along the way, somewhere, somehow, something worked. For caring adults, the bottom line is never quit caring. Never give up on any kid but keep plugging away. Never sway from your beliefs or your standards. You might be surprised how much of a role model you can be for kids who seem to not care. Kids do respect adults who live their values and stick with their beliefs in their daily living. Even those kids who rebel against all adults are very observant of the adults who have talked a good game but live differently and those who show actions consistent with their talk.

As I look back at the many kids I have worked with and the difficult situations in which they lived, it's amazing to realize how many have had resilience to not only survive their situations, but also eventually thrive in a world that seemed very hostile to them. In each of those situations, someone cared, and someone believed in them and helped them set goals far beyond what others expected for them. The key was for them to eventually believe in themselves. Although not all kids I have worked with have made positive choices or have had the opportunities for success, those who have reinforce my belief that kids can, indeed, grow up and be accountable to themselves and be secure in who they have become.

I have been blessed with being able to see many of my kids grow into adulthood and exceed many of the expectations that had been lowered because of their situations, experiences, or disabilities. These kids have oftentimes succeeded despite the many negative influences in their lives and in many cases, because of those few adults who believed in them and helped them believe in themselves. It is heartwarming to see kids who many predicted would never finish high school not only finishing, but also going on to colleges or vocational schools.

It's amazing to me that the chances for success for kids to grow into productive adults is not directly connected to the type or severity of a kid's disability, nor is it always closely related to the socioeconomic status of the kid's family. I have seen kids with childhood autism, severe learning disabilities, moderate developmental disabilities, ADHD, all be successful in living up to their potential. Some went to college and graduate school, and some are working at a sheltered workshop and residing in semi-independent living arrangements. I have seen kids from families of alcoholics, kids who have been physically or sexually abused, kids who have lived in extremely dysfunctional families, and kids who have grown up in poverty, all be successful despite the many obstacles they have faced.

The key ingredient to these kids' success is they have someone—parents, school personnel, parents of friends, church or community people—who have helped them feel worthwhile and modeled effective problem-solving and decision-making for them. At the same time, some have helped them achieve some form of success, whether in academics, sports, or other outside activities. These kids have been taken in by their communities when their families have not been capable of providing for their needs. Another common key ingredient with these kids is each of them could have been seen as "throwaway kids" who had no future or possibility for success. Every time I see one of these grown-up kids, I thank God for the adults in their lives who saw their value and nurtured them in a world that could easily have passed them by. Seeing these grown-up kids continues to reinforce my firm belief that all kids can and should be saved. Regardless of their disability or family situations, each has a special talent and gift, and it is our obligation as adults in their lives to find those gifts and talents and nurture the goodness and worth each of these kids inherently have.

Not all the success stories with kids are with those who were destined for failure or had self-destructive behavior, but some are just situations where kids' lifestyles and life choices are affected by adults who listen and care. One young man spent a considerable amount of time at our home, visiting with my daughters, my wife, and me. Through the years, we always accepted this young man while disagreeing with some of the choices he'd made. We got into many discussions over his values. It was interesting because we never just agreed with his choices, but we also did not put him down. He always came back and continued to be open with us on his feelings and values. Some of the discussions were on religious values, others on work ethic, and some on sexual activity, and others on drug and alcohol use. It finally became apparent to us that he was still searching for his set of values and morals and used us as a sounding board as well as seeing us as role models. When he was a junior in college, he was still searching for career choices, having considered law, medicine, and history. He was still uncertain of which way to go. One spring evening, he showed up at our house to talk with me about a job opportunity he had in an exclusive group home setting on the East Coast with severely disturbed teenagers. I encouraged him to accept the job with the warning that he would either never want to work with kids again or he would have found the direction he was looking for.

That summer was difficult for him, but it was the beginning of a major change in career direction as well as a lifestyle. He has since received a degree in psychology, worked in a group home for developmentally disabled youths, and received a degree as a school psychologist. During this time, he would call to bounce ideas off me, and I have given him job recommendations as well as references for his further education. This young man was not necessarily in danger of ruining his life, but his connection with us has impacted his life. Adults make a difference for kids by listening without judging or controlling but rather by guiding.

A young man diagnosed with childhood autism has attended a local community college and then went on to a four-year college and is now a successful adult. When I first met him, he was in sixth grade, and his prognosis for success was not very good. Although it was obvious he had some academic abilities, his social awkwardness and unusual communication processes made it difficult for him to succeed. He was placed in a special class with integration and received most of his instruction in this classroom. Like many children with autism, he had areas of brilliance he could articulate as if he had a tape in his head that he played. The problem with this is even though he impressed teachers and peers, it really interfered with his communication because he was not interacting but only reciting his knowledge.

The boy had parents who had difficulty accepting his disability, but once they did, they made sure he got testing from experts in the field, and they also received a better understanding of his abilities and capabilities. Because they refused to give up or give in to lesser expectations, they pushed the school to help their son recognize his potential and to have success socially and academically. With the help of special teachers and a talented speech clinician, the young man was taught conversation skills and learned to communicate socially with his peers. Another instructor got him involved in speech where he could use his articulate skills while learning the need for interaction. The bottom line is this was a kid who could have been relegated to simple life skill functioning without utilizing his intelligence and ability. Instead, his parents, teachers, and support people, together with the kid's perseverance and desire to succeed, have allowed this young man to be a successful and happy adult.

A young boy moved into our area from California and brought with him many terrifying memories and fears which often tortured him in frightening nightmares. Because of his traumatic experiences and his failures in his previous schooling, this teenage boy seemed to have more problems than our regular education could handle. He was staffed into special education programming for two reasons: First, we needed to know what his capabilities were, academically and emotionally. Second, we wanted to give him a smaller more structured classroom where he could experience success and feel secure. Although academics were never easy for him, he became involved in a work experience while in high school. He not only graduated, but also became confident enough in his work experience to get a full-time job at a grocery store. He has been there for several years and is now an assistant manager. Although this may not seem like a success story to everyone, for this young man, the outcome could have been so much different if the people around him had not showed him love, respect, care, and stayed with him when he needed security and structure. He never forgets those who cared for him, and he always greets us cheerfully and catches us up on his life. Not that he hasn't made some questionable decisions in his life, but he has learned from his mistakes and seems relatively happy and healthy. Not bad for a kid who seemed to be mentally ill and almost unteachable when he first came to us.

Another kid, who has since grown up, entered my life when he was in fifth grade, when I worked for Lutheran Social Services. He spent a lot of time with my family on our farm. He learned horseback riding and did farmwork with me, shoveling manure from stalls, but more importantly, he learned about work ethics and family pride, feeling a sense of belonging. He came from a family with a single mom and with very little contact with his father. He had two elder brothers: one who had frequently been in trouble with the law, the other had severe developmental delays and struggled with home and academic relationships. This boy became very close to my family and learned many positive ways to deal with life that would later help him through difficult times. Because of the nature of my work, our relationship was intense for a time but then became less and less as the family was functioning better on its own. Years later, I saw him as he was about to start high school, and I found out he had difficulty living down his elder brothers' reputations, and he soon left school. Through the years that followed, I worried about him, but he did keep contact with me from time to time. Eventually, he started to date a young girl from my home school system, who herself had been struggling but was now determined to finish school and be successful. This relationship and perhaps some of the lessons he had learned from our family helped him make changes in his life. He went back for his GED and went to work for an auto parts store in his town. He invited me to his wedding and never forgot the care and love we had shown him. This was an example of someone who made some foolish mistakes but was able to learn from the positive examples in his life, and he was able to be successful in life and relationships.

Not all the kids I have seen as grown-ups have turned out as positive as those I have just described, yet my hope and prayer for each of them is somewhere, somehow, and sometime they too will remember those who cared for them in their lives and follow that positive modeling that was there for them but they chose not to accept it at that time. What is so wonderful is I truly believe it is never too late to make changes in their lives. Even those kids who now are addicted to alcohol or are in prison or are living the same abusive lives they knew as children can make changes if someone important in their lives can reinforce their self-worth and value, leading them to who they can be.

The Special Olympics program is a true example of the worth of those kids, who, even when they grow up, are still kids. Many of the developmentally delayed kids and those with mental disabilities always remain childlike in their intellectual development. These kids do grow up and become adults. The Special Olympics offers a continued opportunity for these kids and adults to grow and develop through sports participation. Many of the participants spend a great deal of time training for their events. For many, it is the chance to do something special that gives meaning to their lives. Many of them also have been able to live semi-independently and work in either shelter workshops. Job coaching or supervision allows them to be productive as adults, even though they may remain childlike in their intellectual functioning. Some of the kids I had worked with in Special Olympics now come back to their school every year and help coach others in swimming, basketball, and track events. They received so much from others that they are eager to give some of that love, care, and reinforcement that have been so important to them. Their self-worth was validated through athletic participation that would not have been available to them except through the Special Olympics program, and now they want to be part of that massive volunteer network that makes the Special Olympics so special. Without participation in Special Olympics and the encouragement of coaches and sponsors, they could very well be inactive adults with little social interaction with their communities.

The other side to watching these special kids grow into adulthood is the wonderful effect these kids have on all the adults in their lives. I thank the Lord every day of my life for the tremendous gifts these kids have given me in terms of recognizing the important things in life, like relationships, honesty, sportsmanship, and true friendship. When these kids let you into their lives, you truly become "friends forever," and when these kids grow up, they never forget you or the caring relationship they have developed with you. I have watched these special kids change the lives of adult teachers, volunteers, and parents with their simplistic philosophy of life and their true sense of friendship and love. They have that simple childlike faith that carries them cheerfully through each aspect their lives.

The alcohol-drug support group I mentioned earlier has certainly brought mixed results as these kids have grown into adulthood. Many of these kids were old well beyond their years when I met them, but their transition to adulthood was still a long and treacherous journey. Some of these kids dropped out of high school, while others struggled through, even after relapses. Some of these kids continued their usage and eventually became involved with law enforcement and, for some, prison. The successes often have been limited by the one-day-at-a-time battle against relapse, and certainly their chance to lead a normal teenage life was taken away from them forever. Nonetheless, many have gone on to college, some have gotten married, and others have successfully entered the work world.

As adults, they have tremendous insight into the world around them. Many have become involved in helping youth make better decisions about drugs and alcohol, speaking to high school, middle school, and church groups. They are also in the precarious position of always carrying their past with them, dealing with the continued pressure of again becoming a user. As difficult as it is for a fifty-year-old adult to face never drinking again, think of how much more difficult it is for a sixteen-year-old or even a twenty-year-old. As these kids become adults, many of the peer activities and entertainment arenas are closed for them. They need to make different and more mature choices. Many of those who succeed have learned the value of their spiritual selves and often find their place in our churches and religious activities. They have learned the perseverance of having to prove themselves to peers and employers who doubt their ability to remain sober and drug free. Although I don't have contact with all my former group members, I see enough of them to know, with proper support and other adults who care, these young people can make the necessary changes in their lives to be successful. I also know those who were not strong enough to resist negative peer influences or who blamed everyone else for their problems in their lives continue to struggle in their lives. As much as it warms my heart to see those who have made the adjustment to adulthood in a positive way, it breaks my heart to see those who did not make that transition as well.

One kid was referred to me in first grade after having drawn a family picture. The man in the drawing had no face. When I got to know the boy, his drawing made perfect sense. He did not know his real father and really had no relationship with him. This kid was already having some behavioral and social issues in class, and the teacher was concerned that he may have a learning disability. Over the years, this boy received considerable teasing from his peers but was quite likeable and got along well with adults. Schoolwork was difficult for him, and he often chose not to do it, even though he was quite capable of doing the work.

His fourth-grade teacher, in her frustration over his unwillingness to do his homework, struck a deal with him that forever changed his life. She agreed to take him to her farm and let him spend time with her family. The catch was he would meet his incentives for doing his work on time. What started out as weekly visits evolved into first doing chores for them and then eventually working on their farm. His teacher and her husband learned, by giving him an opportunity to succeed, his self-worth increased, and the seed was planted that he could be successful as an adult. During this time, his visits to the farm were tied to his schoolwork so he continued to improve at school. During this same time, he also became interested in horses, and during one of our sessions, I invited him to come home with me and do some riding. This also evolved into something very important in his life. He eventually bought a horse and kept it on our acreage. He became a frequent visitor at my place and soon was learning to ride from my daughters. He also followed their lead into 4H and later into FFA. There, he had the opportunity to be in a group setting. From a young boy who seemed very disconnected with male relationships, he became a bright, energetic, and hardworking young man who still means a lot to his farm family and to us. He not only graduated from high school, but has also graduated from college at Iowa State University with a degree in agribusiness. He did not come from a "bad" family but rather a typical one with a single mom who loved her sons but had to work two or three jobs to support her family. It was not that she didn't care, but between the work and other struggles, it was very difficult to give him the time he needed. This was a perfect example of a community working together to raise a child. The young man was considered by many to be a "throwaway child" from the wrong side of the tracks, but now he is a bright, industrious young man who is married and working in his field. He has developed good values in work and life and is being successful.

Believe it or not, all kids do grow up, at least physically, if not mentally or emotionally. When we look at the world around us and see all the crime and immorality and lack of values, it is quite easy to realize not all these kids have grown to be productive adults. To me, this points to an even stronger need for all of us as adults to become involved in that growing process for the kids we work with.

Kids are OK and are all capable of being successful and feeling good about themselves and remaining positive through the adversities of life. Contrary to the belief of many of my peers, who write off kids because of heredity and environment, kids are capable of surviving in the worst of all conditions. Whether kids have parents who are alcoholics, mentally ill, abusive, overindulgent, or incarcerated, kids only need to be able to feel their value as a person and know they have worth and capabilities, and that, my friend, is where we come in. Kids are not born criminals or drug addicts or sexually permissive, but they become what they learn, what have been modeled for them. Kids don't become productive adults by being sheltered from all adversity any more than from being overwhelmed by it. They become strong productive adults by learning appropriate and healthy coping skills. They learn these skills from the positive adults in their lives. A strong old oak tree did not become that way by avoiding and being sheltered from nature's furies. They become strong by enduring all of nature's forces and by sending its roots deep into the earth. Kids also need strong roots to become strong adults to withstand the strong forces of hostility and adversity in their world. These roots come from the many adults who can influence them at home, at school, and in their communities. We don't often know the impact we have on kids as they grow, but trust me, it is solid consistency from adults in their lives that often make that important difference in a child feeling OK about themselves and eventually in making positive choices in their in their journey to adulthood. Even those kids who seemingly have made all the wrong choices and grow into adulthood addicted, in trouble with the law, or without work or education, they can still make changes in their lives. When they do, it is because of some influence of an adult in their lives, at times many years ago.

One good example of planting the seed and seeing it grow into fruition is a successful businessman in one of the communities I worked with in his school. As kid, he had a great personality, with a winning smile and a gift of gab well beyond his years. Unfortunately, he also had a rather severe learning disability and ADHD. Despite his strengths, school was very frustrating and unsuccessful for him. His parents tried to work with the school system, and many attempts were made to motivate him to transfer his people skills and abilities into school success. Bottom line was he couldn't read well, and he couldn't concentrate or focus at all in the classroom. I spent a lot of time with him in school, and we had a good relationship, but in the end, it was not enough. He eventually dropped out of school. At that time, he was a risk-taker and made a lot of questionable choices in his life. What he had going for himself was a good job in his dad's business and his good social skills with customers. Years later, I dealt with him at his business, where he had become the sales manager. When we reminisced about his school difficulties, he admitted to me that he now realized he had a learning disability. He also wanted to go to college for some training in another field, even though he was successful at what he was doing. We talked about his need for extra help and some accommodations; he was willing to accept help now. Years and maturity have helped him see what, as a child, he was unable or unwilling to see. He is successful at what he is doing but still wants to know if he is capable of something else if he chooses to change directions in his life. He asked me if I would be willing to help him while he was in college to find the help he needs. In our conversations, he asked me if I had gotten any better playing UNO. I left that store feeling amazed and more convinced than ever that we can never close the book on kids we have worked with or write them off as unsuccessful. What we need to do is give them the best we can and to let them know they are important and valuable. Sometimes the help we give seems in vain, but we should never get discouraged. Many have become positive and successful adults because of some loving help given to them in their childhood. Kids do grow up, and those of us who have worked in the educational system can be a major factor in that growth.

Chapter Twelve
Study and Discussion Guide

1. Describe kids you have worked with who have seemingly grown up despite themselves.

2. Name some success stories and how adults in their lives have made an impact on their future choices.

3. Reflect on kids who seemed destined for failure but whose resiliency eventually led to their success.

4. How do we know the positive impact we have had on kids as they grow into adulthood?

5. Describe the feeling when a young adult shares how much positive impact you have had on his life.

6. List some of the adults who have had an impact on your life.

THIRTEEN

The Simplicity of Childlike Faith

In a world that exposes children to such atrocities beyond description, it continues to amaze me that kids can still have a very simple faith in their God, their families, and their support systems. Some, of course, are tainted by their circumstances and unable to trust, particularly adults in their lives. Even these children have strong beliefs that their lives will get better. They also have a strong allegiance and loyalty to those they love.

Being a school social worker for over twenty-five years, my business was my kids, and I had countless opportunities for kids to share their innermost feelings and their craziest dreams. The determination and conviction these kids have shown in their beliefs continues to fascinate me. I often had thought, if the adults in their lives still had some of their faith, then the kids would have a good opportunity to keep those wonderful qualities throughout their lives. Somewhere in that transition from childhood to adulthood, something is often lost. Their simple faith vanishes into the dark and suspicious world that they are surrounded by. Rather than look at what can happen, let's continue to look at the amazing resilience and perseverance kids exhibit when faced with difficulties and the faith they have in a positive outcome.

When I think of examples of a kid's faith, I cannot look past my family and a couple of humorous examples from each of my daughter's past. Michelle was five, and Stephanie was two. I was home alone with the girls, and the stillness was suddenly broken by a shrill scream. I went into the living room and found Stephanie had fallen into an end table. She had cracked some teeth and had other facial injuries. I did what I usually would do at the sight of blood—I panicked. I called for Michelle, asking for help, hoping for her to get a wet towel and some bandages. After what seemed to be forever, I picked up Stephanie and went to the bathroom. Michelle was in the bathroom on her knees. I said, "Michelle, I asked you to help."

Michelle's eyes were looking upward toward heaven, and she calmly replied, "I am helping, Daddy, I'm praying to God for Stephanie to get better."

When I calmed down and the situation had been handled, I realized what Michelle did was an example of the faith we had passed on to our girls. She truly "helped."

Another example with my family occurred one Sunday morning, when Stephanie was about four years old. We were attending church and had gone to the front to receive communion. After my wife and I had received the bread and wine, the pastor put his hands on Stephanie's head and gave her a blessing. On her way back to the pew, Stephanie announced in her big voice for all to hear, "God touched me!"

As I think back on that day, I often wonder how many adult lives could be changed if they could so easily sense the presence of God in their lives.

During my career, I often had groups for kids who were dealing with a death in their family. These kids encouraged me with their straightforward and courageous approach to the loss of a loved one. Without exception, these kids would say with absolute resolve their loved ones were living in heaven with God. Even though they would express anger or sadness that this special person had left them, they had no doubt they were now in that special place—heaven; that the person was now content and happy and without pain. It would be easy to dismiss this and to say children just do not understand death, and putting their loved ones in a special fantasy place, heaven, made it easier than dealing with their pain. I have never bought that line of thinking for even one minute. The kids I worked with had a genuine faith in a powerful but loving God who protects their loved ones, even in death. Many of these children would have you believing their pets are also there in heaven. Rather than dismissing this lightly, please remember only God and those who have gone before us really know. What I do know is the simple, easy faith of our kids is a much better coping mechanism than most adults have.

On more than one occasion, I have been taken aback by a child I was counseling. They try to console me, assuring me their mom, dad, grandparent, or sibling are certainly in good hands with God. Not that that they don't show their sadness and sorrow, but those emotions quickly fade in their assurance that their loved ones were, indeed, in a special and happy place. They reminded me of the importance of relying on our faith in our times of sorrow and loss. Their faith could have been the reason why they show such tremendous resiliency and the ability to bounce back quickly in times of sorrow and of loss as well as in times of great stress. They have not yet learned the fear and doubts of their adult counterparts.

Have you ever wondered why many children, especially younger ones, never seem to worry about anything? If you are curious, ask a child, and quite likely, they will tell you they have nothing to worry about. I remember the reply of a six-year-old first-grader to that question: "Why should I worry? I know that I will always be taken care of."

When I asked how he knew that, he responded, "Well, I've got my mom and dad to take care of me at home. I have my older sister to take care of me coming to and from school. I have my teacher to take care of me at school. My friends take care of me at their homes. My pastor takes care of me at church. If any one of them forgets, I've got God who is there to take care of me, so why would I ever worry?"

Why, indeed?

If only we could all live our lives with that assurance that someone is always there to take care of us. Worry is the opposite of faith. The child's simple faith in God and in the people who love him can help him remain calm, knowing he didn't have to become a worrier. It's truly unfortunate that we—parents, educators, and other important people in their lives—often take a child with a simple trusting faith and do everything in our power to make him worry about everything. From criticism over schoolwork to how he cleans his room and how he dresses, to how he is always late in everything he does, we continue to hammer away at our kids and their simple faith until they become like us. Maybe it's time that each of us do the opposite with our kids and learn from them so we may, in turn, regain some of that simplistic faith and trust we lost a long time ago.

One of the most remarkable children I have ever known and worked with for several years was a child with Down's syndrome. Even as she grew physically and in years, her developmental age remained that of a child. This young lady had an outlook on life that had to bring a smile to the crassest cynic. She had a smile that warmed the heart and a strong will that would very directly let you know what she wanted. If I've ever known a child with a direct pipeline to God, it had to be her. She had a way of endearing herself to others that I have rarely seen before or since. To have a personal relationship with her meant "friends for life." Once she trusted you, she knew in her heart her trust would never be violated. Although she spent most of her school time in a special classroom with six to eight other children with developmental disabilities, she became known to the entire school population. They would often share their lunchtime or other free time with her. She rarely missed an athletic event and always knew the scores of all the games. Her parents acknowledged her gifts and actively directed her in many people-oriented activities. This friend of mine died at a very young age, but she left a legacy of faith and love for all who knew her. When I think of this simple day-to-day living faith, I think of her life, and even though I miss her, I know she is sharing that same wondrous gift with others in heaven.

It's interesting that in a time when prayer and Christian traditions or other God-centered activities are banned from our school systems, I have learned more about faith, prayer, and belief from the children I worked with than that time I worked for a faith-based agency. Although we cannot present faith in our teaching or counseling, thankfully, no one can prevent the children for bringing it with them. Whether I was in the classroom teaching listening skills, in a small group working on social skills, or working individually with a child, their simple faith rings clearly in their participation in whatever activities we were doing. Their faith and trust leave them with a sense of innocence but also vulnerability. It is important the adults in their lives reinforce their simple faith rather than take advantage of their vulnerability.

In my position, I was often called upon when a tragedy of a child's death occurs in one of the schools I worked in. Over the years, I have seen this simple faith in middle school and high school students who come out in a time of crisis. On one occasion, when one of their classmates was hospitalized in critical condition and another was killed, I learned much about faith from those students. Not only did their faith shine strongly through their grief over the loss of their friend and classmate, but also in their steadfast faith in God that their friend in the hospital could and would recover. It was the first time in a non-church setting that I felt the power of prayer, as I counseled with and consoled the more than sixty students in the high school that day of the accident. Their assurance that their friend, who had been killed, was now without pain and with their God in heaven was comforting to the parents and the school staff. It's amazing, when youth face a crisis, their faith supersedes all other feelings and emotions. These kids were confused and uncertain about the events that occurred but nonetheless, strengthened by their faith, volunteered to be pallbearers at her funeral. They amazed the clergy and funeral director with their maturity and understanding. In the weeks to come, they neither forgot their lost classmate nor their hospitalized friend. Many of the students visited the cemetery daily to feel the closeness with her. They also prayed daily and kept in contact with the other classmate's parents as he continued to be in critical condition. When he started his recovery and was no longer in danger, these students prayed together and gave thanks for his recovery. Throughout this ordeal, these students showed no doubt that God's presence was with them, helping them deal with their grief. They also knew their prayers were heard and answered in the healing of their injured friend. This certainly was not a part of my job that I looked forward to, yet it was another time I learned about the faith of the kids I worked with. If we sometimes doubt the values and faith of our youth, particularly our teenagers, that doubt melts away quickly as we see their response to tragedy and crisis. That simple faith is still there; it is just not as acceptable to show it or practice it like when they were younger. That's sad but true and points again to our need as adults to be models of that faith so that simple faith of our childhood does not have to be buried or even lost forever. In the thirty years I worked closely with kids, I have seen innumerable examples of simple, childlike faith in kids from ages three to twenty-three. I have marveled at their undaunted courage and energy as they face their lives. Many of these children have had more obstacles to overcome than we will see in a lifetime. They have had that remarkable perseverance and resilience helped by their beliefs and their faith in those who care for them and in their God. I am convinced their simple faith is the key to successful living for them. It can act as a buffer through their many difficulties and gives them the strength to sustain them in their many struggles. As parents and educators, we need to recognize this faith in our children and to nurture and encourage its development. I know in my heart, if we destroy this faith through our unrealistic expectations and our criticism toward them, we are taking away the greatest gift they have—a gift they freely share.

Chapter Thirteen
Study and Discussion Guide

1. Give examples of how faith can be a comfort for young children who are grieving.

2. Why are children so resilient in their ability to cope with death and other trauma in their lives?

3. Why do adults seem to avoid faith in dealing with their difficulties?

4. Children can at times be helpful for adults who are struggling with their faith issues. Give some examples.

5. Simplicity is not to be confused with easy. Children still struggle with grief issues but seem to have better coping skills than many adults. Discuss.

FOURTEEN

May There Always Be a Child in Each of Us

If there has ever been an effective prescription for health and happiness, it is "Live your life with all your heart, your soul, and your ability; laugh and smile a lot; and never forget that inner child that allows you to experience every day with a sense of innocence and freshness so you can the best that you can possibly be. We can reduce the stress and strain of daily living by getting in touch with our inner child. It enables us to live easier and more comfortably. It also helps us let go of the unimportant, discarding the unnecessary garbage and baggage we often carry through life, trying to live up to everyone else's expectations. For those of us who have spent their lives around kids, we know that tremendous sense of enthusiasm for life that only the innocence of youth can experience. That inner child has often been numbed and desensitized as we have grown to be adults. It is that desire to experience and to live each moment, seeing all of nature's beauty and life's wonderful surprises. I believe, as adults, how we experience our world greatly affects our attitude and ability to cope with its adversity. If we can allow our inner child to be a vital part of our personality, we can cope with what life deals us.

As a child, I remember certain television personalities who utilized their ability to retain that inner child and turned it into successful career. Those stars who come to mind are Red Skelton, Lucile Ball, Jerry Lewis, and Bob Hope. I remember being uncomfortable seeing grown-ups acting so silly and immature, yet there was something special about their lack of inhibitions and the willingness to be different from their peers. Although much of their humor was slapstick, childish behavior, there was a certain freshness and innocence as well as being funny. A common trait among these celebrities was that twinkle in their eyes, denoting a true enjoyment of life. There was also a childlike sense of joy in their fun-filled antics. It was interesting for me to see adults acting in this way, yet there was no sense of embarrassment or guilt over their behavior. I remember, as I was growing up, many adults would rarely, if ever, crack a smile. Certainly, we were taught to never do anything humiliating or downgrading, like acting out our inner child.

These comedians made millions of people laugh, but more importantly, they taught me that we can laugh at ourselves and let down the many walls that have been erected and be ourselves. That means allowing the child within us to play and be part of our being. You may think these and other comedians were just acting, yet their whole demeanor and way of presenting themselves strongly indicated their childlike behavior and actions we saw were real and humorous. Their slapstick silliness and funny interactions were fun for them and were part of allowing themselves to retain that inner child in their personalities.

In our adult world, acting like a child seems to carry a negative connotation, like the person hasn't grown or is being irresponsible or irreverent. It is often looked down upon for an adult to be silly and bubbly or even to become excited or exuberant out in the world with people around him. Restraint and constraint seem to be the acceptable behavior of adults, but what a shame that is. If we don't keep that "child within," we miss out on a great deal fun and experiences only the "kid" in us will risk having. We also fail to connect or interact with our children. We deny that child within us that will allow our understanding that helps us relate to all the kids in our lives. Being in touch with our kid does not mean being childish or behaving improperly, nor does it mean having our kids as peers or our friends. What it does mean is remembering how it feels to be a kid, the wonderful positives as well as the devastating negatives. Remembering the intensity of the experience and the sense of timing only kids can understand can help us see the teachable moments with our kids and to be there at times when we can make a difference in their lives. It also helps us remember the emotions of our youth and acknowledge them with our kids normalizing the many ups and downs they naturally go through. If we can stay connected with our child, maybe we can become more tolerant and accepting in our dealings with the kids in our lives.

In the thirty years I worked with children, I had the opportunity to meet and get to know some remarkable people of all ages and backgrounds. Some of the most common traits they all shared were their abilities to be playful, cheerful, and fun-loving in their dealing with the people they worked with. One of the most wonderful people I met was the noted author of many books in the field of psychology and holistic therapeutic methods, Virginia Satir. I met her at a workshop about five years prior her death. At that time, she was nearing the end of her long career of helping and caring for people. I was moved by her kindness and sensitivity but also by that wonderful twinkle in her eyes that showed a sense of playfulness and joy that I knew were part of her inner child, which was still vibrant inside of her. I got a hug from Virginia, and that sense of freshness and excitement with the world around her gave me a new direction in the therapeutic sense as well as the personal. Part of her tremendous insight into people was her understanding of that child within us all and the need for each of us to remain in touch with our inner child. Although I had previously read many of her books, they really became alive in me after I had met her personally. Shortly after that encounter, I became a school social worker. Many of her methods of relating to kids were helpful for me in the school setting. I remember her premise that we need to understand and relate to those we work with. If we cannot get in touch with our child, then helping children becomes even more difficult.

Maintaining the kid within ourselves often gives us the ability to laugh at our shortcomings and be more accepting and sensitive to the shortcomings of others. It helps us continue to be excited and enthusiastic about each coming moment. Often kids are criticized for not sharing their feelings. Yet it is usually because they model after their parents and other adults who have presented the model of being closed, secretive, and wary of letting others into their lives. If we wish for kids to learn to enjoy and nurture that fun-loving and innocent part of them, then we, adults, must continue to nurture the same within ourselves.

Many times adults, particularly teachers, receive a bad rep as only being concerned about a child becoming responsible and obedient and that they are not sensitive to their emotional and social needs. I'd like to share an unfortunate incident that certainly brought negative reaction toward teachers. My youngest daughter was seven and in second grade at the time. She went to school on a Monday morning quite upset because her kitten had died the night before. When she returned home that afternoon, we were angry and appalled to find that her teacher told her it was inappropriate for her to cry and that if she couldn't handle her emotions, she should have stayed home. Despite reassurance from us that her feelings were real and normal and that sharing them with others was OK, it was a long time before she was willing to share her feelings with a supposedly safe adult. After twenty-five years in the school system, I know that a high percentage of our teachers recognize the importance of any loss in a child's life. They call upon their child within and have for their kids. They are also willing to risk sharing themselves with their kids in relating to the many wonders of childhood that unfolds before their eyes when kids are allowed to be kids and not little adults or obedient robots.

It was not easy for me seek the "kid" in myself. I am forever grateful to the many wonderful kids and teachers who taught me how to share that part of myself with others. It has given me the freedom to be myself and to accept the joy of sharing moments of happiness and moments of sadness and sorrow with those kids whose life I share. That same feeling of discomfort I had as a child watching Red Skelton and Jerry Lewis returned to me when I started working with young children and the situation called for more silliness and risk-taking. Thankfully, I realized I could not expect children to risk being silly or sharing if I was unwilling to model that behavior for them. I thank God every day that He helped me choose to show all my kids I was a person who could be silly or embarrassed, make mistakes, and even laugh with others at myself. That choice has helped me grow so much as a person and opened my heart to the wonderful world of kids.

One college professor I had made a lasting impression upon me by his unique ways of getting and holding our attention. This man was probably in his forties, was short, plump, and bald-headed. He was trying to teach economics to college students at eight o'clock in the morning. It brings a smile to my face even now to think of this man imitating a steam engine and puffing his away around the room, complete with noises, including a bell and whistle. Another time he taught us about the rising inflation by pretending to be an airplane and rising from the floor upward with his arms outstretched like wings. While I don't remember a lot about economics (but yes, I did pass), I'll never forget him as a person. He had fun with life and was not afraid to throw away his inhibitions and thoroughly entertain the class as he taught. Like others I have mentioned, his eyes sparkled, and his demeanor was one of delight and enjoyment. His "kid inside" was obviously alive and well.

Another person who never let the "kid" in her retreat very far beneath the surface was a wonderful speech and language pathologist who did classroom groups with me for two years before she retired. She found more ways to bring humor and laughter to the classroom than anyone I have ever known. Whether it was using her puppet dog or her puppet pig, Cool Running, or a myriad of other puppets and accessories, she always brought smiles to the faces of the kids while teaching lessons in social skills. I spent most of those two years playing the "straight guy" for her many antics and enjoying every minute of it. She was uninhibited in her work with children, reaching inside to her child in a playful and at times very sensitive way. She knew how to draw out the shy child and how to disarm the smart aleck and how to give "warm fuzzes" to everyone. She and I put together a manual for teaching social skills in the classroom for kindergarten and first through fourth grades. We were asked to present our methods and manual at the annual school social work conference. That's when she showed me her wonderful ability to draw the child out of anyone. Presenting to a group of forty social workers and one psychologist, my boss, she had them just as involved and entertained as any first-grader we presented to. Using my boss as our prime target, we had the entire audience role-playing, singing, and playfully going along with her antics. That wonderful playful child within her was contagious, and anyone who wants to catch the moment only needs to be in contact with their inner child. For many years after she retired, kids would ask me about my funny friend and say they miss her. They also remember and practice many of the skills we taught them.

Guidance counselors in our schools are given the huge responsibility to relate to and offer assistances to any of the children who need help in their buildings. That usually is between 25 and 50 percent of the kids in their charge. Because of the large numbers, many counselors do classroom groups or other small groups to have contact with all their students. Many programs are available to the counselors, but almost all of them involve puppets or stuffed animals or other props to use. If counselors are not comfortable with methods of play in groups, they probably will not last long.

Picture a rather large lady with a gruff voice bringing an equally large teddy bear into her classroom and using the bear to tell stories to her kids. This dear friend of mine would seem to be least likely to reach inside and use her "playful kid" to reach her kids. She does, however, do it with ease and skill and has fun doing it. This counselor is also the most skilled grief counselor I have worked with. Through her tragic experiences, she has learned what kids need to deal with loss in their lives. Her ability to laugh and joke with her students also allows her to relate to them when they need help with their grief.

Another friend of mine was so adept at using his "kid" that I often wonder if he ever grew up. He could often be seen walking in the halls with his two billed baseball cap that says, "I'm their leader, which way did they go?" He could make me laugh more than any other person I know. Together, our "kids" ran wild. Doing groups and classroom guidance with him is a real delight. Whether using Duso the Dolphin, teaching the kids to line-dance, or demonstrating how to duck walk, we always have the kids' undivided attention. This is also the only person I know who could get his freshman boys basketball team to let down their guard and sing a silly song before each game. He was contagious, and everyone who had the opportunity to catch his beautiful, fun-filled personality has grown from it. Yet like many other skilled counselors I work with, they use their "kid" to help sensitize them to the kids they work with. Our counselors are often underestimated and underappreciated, yet they do wonders with the many kids who need a friend, who can understand, listen, and help. Unfortunately, many school personnel still have difficulty understanding how playing games and laughing can be helpful to these kids. Over the years, all of us who work closely with kids have worked hard to change those attitudes.

One of my coworkers was the epitome of a powerful and sensitive counselor. He has now received training and is a certified play therapist now working in a local agency. He took the role of the "kid" to another level. He is delightful, kind, and a gentleman who cares. He has a unique ability to allow himself to relate to kids on a level they can understand and trust. In the school setting, he would physically get on the level with his kids to listen to them and to give and receive hugs. He could giggle and be silly or become overly serious until one of his kids start laughing, which brings a smile back to his face. He has become skilled in working with kids who have been abused in different ways. He gains their trust so they can make their journey back to being healthy again. He was my mentor and my friend, and that wonderful "kid" inside of him brought me many laughs and at times some tears when we worked with kids together.

Although I have highlighted some of the counselors who showed, time after time, the importance of finding and using their "kid" in their work and their lives, I don't mean to neglect the many teachers who utilize that "kid" within in them in their classroom work with their kids. All of us from age three to ninety-three have that wonderful, playful, honest, and innocent child inside us. Each one of us can help life be more fun and enjoyable, making the most difficult day more tolerable.

It is so important that we all will be the best possible person we can be in life. We cannot achieve that without the sensitivity and love of that child within us. Life can be too serious, and we need to lighten it up with laughter. We need to approach life as an adventure as only a child can do. Kids have taught me many lessons over the past thirty years, but the most important one of all is that a child is a wonderful blessing to each of us, and we are entrusted with their well-being and nurturing so each child has a chance to grow into a sensitive and caring adult who never forgets their child within.

I realize I have only touched the tip of the iceberg. I hope this sample of the many ways kids affect our lives will help us have the energy, sensitivity, and love to go underneath that tip of the iceberg and see what lies in store for all of us.

Chapter Fourteen
Study and Discussion Guide

1. How can keeping a childlike view of the world be helpful for all of us?
2. Laughter should always be part of who we are in our lives. Talk about the importance of laughter in your life.
3. We should never forget the joy of childlike experiences we can still enjoy. Name several of them.
4. The child in us can give us the courage to go down new avenues in our daily living. Has this ever happened to you?
5. Nothing is more fun than to enjoy activities with our kids. Describe times this happens with kids in your life.

FIFTEEN

Our Work with Kids Is Never Done

As I said at the end of the last chapter, we've only uncovered the tip of the iceberg in understanding kids and their behavior. No matter what we have done or accomplished with kids, there is always so much more to do. While we still have learning disabilities going undiagnosed, and kids with multiple disabilities not being dealt with, then our work with kids is only beginning and is a long way from being complete. When we still keep kids with developmental disabilities away from the general population in our schools and fail to involve them in community activities they could use in adult settings, then we are doing a disservice to them. While bullying is still prevalent in our schools and appropriate measures and programs to deter it have not been implemented, then many of our students will continue to be harmed emotionally and sometimes physically. We also will not solve the bullying problems until we deal with the bullies and what motivates them and their behavior. They can be changed with appropriate training and motivation. When we find the underlying reasons why kids become bullies, then intervention is possible to change their attitudes and beliefs. Many of the problems and difficulties our children encounter in our schools are not going to be changed or alleviated until each school and every employee becomes involved in a positive behavior support program for all our students.

Every year in my schools, as well as in schools across our country, many students reach the level of despair that they consider taking their lives. Many of the senseless tragedies could be prevented if our kids were given knowledge and information about suicide and the reasons behind those decisions. Students can be taught strategies to deal with depression, grief and loss, despair, and loneliness in ways they could see alternatives to taking their lives. Students can also be given the resources so contacts are made available to them to help them through the times of depression and suicidal ideations and give them the needed help to guide them to healthier decisions. The old saying "Suicide is a permanent solution to a temporary problem" is true for each of us today. We need to understand our feelings and deal with them in a way that will help us continue living. That way, we can find positive outcomes to our problems and difficulties.

One of the area education agencies where I worked developed a "Suicide Prevention Taskforce." It was made up of all the school social workers in the agency. Our goal was to develop a program that would help all teachers and other school employees gain the knowledge and skills to help deal with the problem of suicide within their schools. Our team went out to every district in our AEA, either individually or in groups, and presented our program to all school employees. This included classroom aides, teacher associates, bus drivers, secretaries, and all coaches. Our bottom line was we wanted every school employee in our AEA to be given the knowledge to help recognize suicidal symptoms and ideations and to have the skills to take appropriate actions that help prevent tragedies from happening.

Trauma teams and crisis intervention teams are extremely important in our schools. Unfortunately, they usually deal with tragedies and disasters after they happen. The suicide prevention team could prevent some of those tragedies from becoming a reality.

Other district-wide programs on bullying, dropout prevention, and realistic drug and alcohol intervention could also be effective preventative measures that could reduce the frequency and severity of trauma within our districts.

Every child in our care deserves an opportunity for success. It is our responsibility in the education field to help make that happen in any way we can. A child is not going to be successful unless they have the confidence and assurance that they are capable of being successful in an area they are interested in. Guidance counselors and social workers can be extremely helpful in showing students their area of strengths and helping them get the training needed to become skilled in those areas. Lots of times students do not realize their ability levels or their areas of interest until they are given knowledge and training and instruction in different areas so they can decide which areas are right for them. In addition to educational training, educators can help direct kids into various areas of interest. Some may have the ability to excel in sports, others in music. Kids may have a talent in writing or in acting or in debating. It is those of us in education who can help direct kids into their areas of interest and talent and then become their biggest cheerleaders as they reach success in those areas. Kids are defined by what they can be and who they are. We, educators, can help them find the answers to what is right for them and how they can define success for themselves and not be dependent on others. Every child should have someone who cares enough to help guide them in a direction that is right for them and then help them have the confidence to attain their goals. All kids are like birds who leave the nest and learn how to fly by themselves. As adults in their lives, we need to be the winds beneath their wings, allowing them to gain confidence in their abilities. We need to allow our kids to be successful at whatever fits for them.

This certainly is not a solution to all the areas of needs our children have. It is at least a beginning point where parents, teachers, counselors, pastors, and all other adults can build on as we all try to give our kids the best opportunity for success as kids and later as adults. Everyone needs to be in this together, showing our care and compassion and sharing all our knowledge so our kids know we care and are there for them every step of the way. We may still be at the tip of the iceberg, but at least we can be making progress along the way.

Our goal is to find that pot of gold at the rainbow's end. That is where all our kids have the opportunity "to be the best they can be." Until we get there, everyone in education needs to continue to help kids in any way we can. Eventually, we will find that rainbow's end, and our kids will be successful in life, and we will have helped them get there.

Chapter Fifteen
Study and Discussion Guide

1. Talk about issues that have not been dealt with in this book.
2. How can bullying be prevented at school and in the workplace?
3. Describe how we can continue to even the playing field for people with disabilities.
4. As educators, how can we continue to advocate for our kids in all settings?
5. Kids should never be forgotten or put down. Describe programs that now exist that can help kids with their self-esteem in finding their identities.

Printed in the United States
by Baker & Taylor Publisher Services